THE ORDER OF THINGS

JAMES V. SCHALL

THE ORDER OF THINGS

IGNATIUS PRESS SAN FRANCISCO

Cover art: Master Bertram, *The Creation of the Animals.*
Panel from the Grabow Altarpiece at the St. Petri Church in Hamburg, 1379–1383.

Cover design by John Herreid

ISBN 978-1-58617-197-1
Library of Congress Control Number 2006939355
Printed in the United States of America ♾

Isn't it one great predicament not to let them [potential philosophers] taste of arguments while they are young? I suppose you aren't unaware that when lads get their first taste of them, they misuse them as though it were play, always using these to contradict and imitating those men by whom they are refuted. They themselves refute others, like puppies enjoying pulling and tearing with argument at those who happen to be near. . . . Then when they themselves refute many men and are refuted by many, they fall quickly into a profound disbelief of what they formerly believed. And as a result of this, you see, they themselves and the whole activity of philosophy become the objects of slander among the rest of men.

—Plato *Republic* 539b–c

The voyage which I was born to make in the end, and to which my desire has driven me, is towards a place in which everything we have known is forgotten, except those things which, as we knew them, remind us of an original joy.

—Hilaire Belloc, "The Harbour in the North",
in *Hills and the Sea*, 218–19

As the Philosopher says in the beginning of the *Metaphysics*, it is the business of the wise man to order. The reason for this is that wisdom is the highest perfection of reason, whose characteristic is to know order. Even if the sensory powers know something absolutely, nevertheless, it belongs to the intellect or reason alone to know the order of one thing to another. Now, a twofold order is found in things. One, of parts of a whole or of a multitude among themselves, as parts of a house are mutually ordered to one another. The second order is that of things to an end. This order is of greater importance than the first. . . .

Now order is related to reason in a fourfold way. There is one order that reason does not establish but only considers, such as the order of things in nature (metaphysics, physics). There is a second order that reason, in considering, establishes in its own act; for example, when it arranges its concepts among themselves and the signs of concepts, since they are sounds that signify something (logic). There is a third order that reason, in considering, establishes in the operations of the will (ethics). There is a fourth order that reason, in considering, establishes in the external things that it produces, like a chest and a house (art or craft).

—Thomas Aquinas, prologue,
commentary on Aristotle's *Ethics*, 1

True philosophy deals with everything that is given, within as well as without.... Our longing for knowledge is indeed beyond our control. Is this not what Plato had in mind when he compared the philosopher to the lover? The philosopher, too, is "beside himself" because he is moved to the core by the *mirandum*, the wonder of the world.

—Josef Pieper, *In Defense of Philosophy*, 16–17

Those who read great works . . . will read the same work ten, twenty or thirty times during the course of their life.

—C. S. Lewis, *An Experiment in Criticism*, 2

Contents

Preface

> I have at last finished my *Lives* [*of the Poets*], and have laid up for you a load of copy, all out of order, so that it will amuse you a long time to set it right. Come to me, my dear Bozzy, and let us be as happy as we can. We will go again to the Mitre, and talk old times over.
>
> —Samuel Johnson to James Boswell, March 14, 1781[1]

The main theme of this book is found in this brief passage from a letter of Samuel Johnson, the great English lexographer and philosopher, to the Scottish lawyer James Boswell. This same Boswell, of course, wrote what is still the best and most fascinating biography in the English language about this very extraordinary Englishman, Samuel Johnson. Things playful and lightsome are found in this passage. We discover a spirit here that I hope will also be found in the pages to follow. We find also a soberness here, a reminder of our human condition seen in its passingness, yet spoken of in fondness. Much of our lives are spent in setting things out-of-order aright, but only after first understanding that they are in fact out of order.

Johnson had just chided Boswell for being overly pompous and speaking of high-sounding principles like "Liberty and Necessity" when Boswell meant only that he is coming to visit Johnson. Boswell regularly returned each year to London from Scotland to spend some time with Johnson. This year, in 1781, they were to meet at the famous tavern the Mitre, where they would talk "old times over".

[1] *Boswell's Life of Johnson* (London: Oxford, [1799] 1931), 2:386.

This is the great human freedom, to reflect on the past times of our lives and how they were spent so as not to forget them. Johnson was now an old man. He died three years later, on December 13, 1784.

Johnson tells the younger man that they will seek to "be as happy as we can". We are given some happiness in this life, to be sure. That happiness is not to be denigrated. But Johnson, the great moralist, is aware that such happiness as we find, though real, is limited. When Johnson was forty years old, he wrote his famous *The Vanity of Human Wishes, Being the Tenth Satire of Juvenal.* He already felt this poignancy of our lot: "Year chases year; decay pursues decay, / Still drops some joy from with'ring life away; / New forms arise, and diff'rent views engage, / Superfluous lags the vet'ran on the stage, / And bids afflicted worth retire to peace" (lines 305–10). The order of the years, even decay, follows a path, but hints of joy remain, a time to begin and retire, to live and die.

Johnson gives Boswell copies or galleys of his massive lives of English poets, finally finished. But alas, the pages are "out of order". He hopes that Boswell will find some amusement for a long time to "set the pages right". Johnson is obviously confident that Boswell can in fact set the pages right, that is, that he can see some order in them, some logic that binds one page to the next in a manner to make the whole intelligible to the reader.

I take this scene to be a symbol of our lives, of our attempts to put order into things that seem to be out of order. I have heard parents, to correct their little children in some rant of childhood misbehavior, tell them, "You are out of order." A good part of parenthood is consumed in the effort to put order into the souls of children. Children soon learn what order is and eventually understand that the parents knew what they did not yet know. They also learn that they can choose not to follow the reprimand, hence again evoking the said "out of order" command.

We would not be amiss, as we shall see, to notice that this possibility of *non serviam*, of "I shall not serve", is in Scripture. It is the main disorder of the creature known as Satan. It also describes something about ourselves. Evidently, order in certain areas of reality must itself be freely chosen. But if order is rejected, as it can be, it is always rejected in the name of another order, even if it be one that has no origin except in ourselves. The great Augustine called it "pride" when we see no order in the universe except that which we construct for ourselves.

We see signs on elevators and other mechanical devices indicating that they are "out of order". We know what this information means. "The dang things don't work." We know of people whose lives lack order, something we could not affirm unless we had some prior notion of what order might consist in. We constantly hear that the universe itself, according to some scientists, reveals no order, even though the Greek word "cosmos" means that it has an order, a relation of parts to a whole. Some philosophers and theologians even wonder whether order is found in the origin of things, whatever that origin may be. Others deny the possibility of "original order".

We cannot help but be puzzled by all of this order and disorder speculation. Are we perhaps the only beings in the universe without order? Or is everything in chaos? If there is no order, why do we attempt to put some order into things? Why does anything work anyhow? The computer fascinates us because it is a machine that tries to anticipate the moves that we might make that are out of prescribed order, moves that cause it not to work. We can put in a series of ten or twelve letters or numbers, and lo, the computers find what we want to find.

If we miss one letter or number, nothing happens, or some wrong item appears. And we know that what appears is not what we were looking for or intending. It seems strange that we have minds that seem to recognize the difference between order and disorder, between things that work and things that do not. We know that our minds were not made by ourselves, yet they function. We have to be curious about this.

Each of the chapters in this book will ask about some level or aspect of order. The very question of order obviously comes immediately from Aristotle and Aquinas, who pointed out the various orders that the mind is open to knowing or considering. Aristotle remarked that a doctor does not cure us. Nature cures us. The doctor's function is to remove what prevents the body from doing its own repair work. Or he supplies a substitute for what is not working, something that can take the place of what nature originally provided—a hearing aid or eyeglasses, for example. To do either of these functions—to remove or repair—the doctor must know what the normal functioning of the body in health is. This normalcy he does not himself create but finds already, as it were, working in human beings.

So let us inquire about order and, yes, disorder in the various areas of reality in which they appear. If we are to understand a thing, we need first to know what it is, then invoke or seek its causes—why it is this and not that? What brought it into being? Out of what is it made? For what end does it function? But this book is not content only to ask questions. To ask a question is to expect an answer, even when the answers do not seem sufficient or prove to be wrong. To be content with asking questions without seeking answers, without ever knowing or recognizing any answers to any questions, is a form of scepticism, not intelligible order.

These chapters proceed step by step. We consider the basic questions of order in the Godhead, the cosmos, the soul, the polity, and the mind, as well as in hell, in redemption, and in beauty. Things are related both to one another and to their origins and destinies. The human mind is designed to know the truth, even when we choose not to know it because we suspect that it might interfere with the order we choose to put into our own souls, where the ultimate drama, hence order, in the universe ultimately lies.

But the very fact that we can choose to put a disorder into the highest things about us indicates that an order exists by which we can and do distinguish order and disorder. We are beings, as Aristotle said, for whom praise and blame are constant companions. Praise and blame have to do with order and disorder. If things fit together, if they belong together, we want to know how and why. This seeking is our glory. But we do not seek just to be seeking. We seek to know, to know the answers, to know the truth of things. This too is what order is about.

CHAPTER I

THE ORDERLY AND THE DIVINE

"Or do you [Adeimantus] suppose there is any way of keeping someone from imitating that which he admires and therefore keeps company with?"

"It's not possible", he said.

"Then it's the philosopher, keeping company with the divine and the orderly, who becomes orderly and divine, to the extent that is possible for a human being."

—Plato *Republic* 500c–d

I

While in a hospital waiting for an examination, I found a copy of an old, but elegant, *Architectural Digest*. On one of the glossy ad pages, I noticed the following *New Yorker* cartoon by S. Gross. A large cat is depicted determinedly walking on his two hind legs. He is pulling a little toy car on a long string. In the car sits a happy little mouse at the steering wheel. But behind the car, we see another mouse furiously yelling at the contented mouse in the toy car, "For God's sake, think! Why is he being so nice to you?" Notice the second mouse's commands: "Think!" "For God's sake!" It is as if, in our expressions, we realize that we are not just to think but are commanded to think by what is the cause of our being, the kind of being that includes thinking. Thinking means separating this thing from that.

It means identifying accurately what each thing is. It means relating this thing to that. It means seeing the order of how this thing stands to that thing.

Much of what this book is about can be found in this amusing cat-and-mouse scene. The cat is being a cat, being what-it-is-to-be a cat. Nothing is different here about the cat. But the little mouse ought to know what cats do. The mouse in the toy car is, however, happy to have a fun ride. The cat, he thinks, is doing him a favor. He is on a joyride. He is delighted with the unaccustomed experience. We, the viewers, however, know the relation of cats and mice.

The rational mouse's cry to his friend in the car is the voice of intelligence: "Why is he being so nice to you?" That is, the cat's goodness isn't natural. Cats play with mice only to devour them when they get tired of playing games. If they can, mice flee cats on sight. The little mouse in the toy car doesn't get it. Here lies the humor of the cartoon. We see it because we have minds. We see relationships. We see order and therefore the unexpected disorder out of which humor arises. We know that at least one mouse is not being mouselike, or, from our viewpoint, rational.

We get the point. To understand what this cartoon is about, we need to understand what mice and cats do when they are being what they are. An implicit order is presupposed in the cartoon. Since only human beings understand cartoons, we respond to this scene with bemused laughter because we know the order and see, at the same time, the disorder. We can only laugh when we see the incongruity in the scene.

If, however, as in the famous painting *The Peaceable Kingdom* by Edward Hicks, the lion and the lamb, the cat and the mouse do recline together in harmony with no fear of danger, there would be no joke. And if there is no joke, no world as we know it is seen in the painting, even though there may be some other order in the Peaceable Kingdom. The very point in such a Kingdom is that this harmonious scene does not happen in this world, the one we know. Our laughter depends on our seeing the incongruity of things. We see such incongruity only when we simultaneously see the congruity of things.

II

In this same hospital waiting room, I was asked, before the doctor could proceed, to read and sign a waiver, sometimes known, humorously, as "signing your life away". The official document explained that I was a patient. I was to agree that certain procedures were to be performed on me if the doctor judged them necessary. I was told that I might need a transfusion. But what particularly impressed itself on my mind was the statement that the hospital wanted me to know that "medicine was not an exact science", something I confess to having suspected.

Things might go wrong, in other words, in spite of the best efforts of the doctors and the hospital. They wanted me, the patient, to know that possibility. Here was a fleeting intimation of another order over which the hospital as such had no control, or even information about. Neither the doctor nor the hospital, as such, was directly concerned with the ultimate purpose of my life. They were properly concerned only with the present condition of my bodily health. To find out about "ultimate purposes", I would have to go elsewhere—to the philosophers, perhaps, or to wise men, or to the law and the prophets.

Until I consented, however, neither the doctor nor the hospital could legally proceed to do anything to me, even for my own good. This waiver did not mean, of course, that doctors were free to do whatever they wanted with their patients. They could be held for malpractice in glaring cases of not following ordinary medical rules and procedures. But medical science knows things only "for the most part". The human being, indeed any limited being, can vary in individual cases, which are not always covered by general norms. This particular possibility is why the waiver is needed. Not everything can be foreseen, though at times, we wonder about that. We wonder about our finiteness. We wonder if everything should be foreseen, yet not predetermined. These are legitimate questions of theodicy and philosophy, the relation of free will and providence.

So again here, as in the case of the cat and the mouse, we are to understand the nature of a human being and of the medical profession's relation to him. An order of health exists, however much in some things it may vary in particulars from individual to individual. Sickness presupposes health, which sickness did not invent. Health, if you will, invented sickness, or at least the comparative knowledge of what it is.

The doctor does not constitute the requirements of "what it is to be healthy" in the first place. He is a servant of a health he does not himself first make or define. He has to find out what health is by experience, by study of actual human beings. His knowledge does not fall down from the clouds. The doctor who does not seek to make us healthy by standards to which he is obligated is, as Plato already knew, a dangerous man. We do not go to a doctor who is our sworn enemy or to one who refuses to be bound by the standards of what it is to be healthy and how to restore that condition.

We know many things about how to keep healthy and how to restore ourselves when we are sick. Besides modern medicine, working at this same issue of health, are all the health food stores, traditional medicines, prayers for the sick, exercise programs, and, yes, a multitude of quacks. But still the solemn warning of medical science goes out to the patient. We are not an exact science. Do not expect miracles. Miracles are not our business, even if they happen on our watch. We know a lot, but the risk that the patient takes is that we do not know everything. The probability is that we know enough to cure the patient's immediate problem. So go ahead, take the risk. Chances of success are quite realistic, probably more so than if we do nothing.

Some things are not entirely possible for human beings, even for doctors. This lack of "entire" possibility, be it noted in the beginning, is not a bad thing. Life in part consists of lists of what is possible and what is not. The list is variable. We once thought it impossible to walk on the moon, or to use a phone without wires, or to have a tooth pulled without much pain. It is all right that we be the kind of finite beings we are. Yet, as Aristotle told us in a famous passage, we should strive with all our might to know not merely mortal things, but the highest things. We are to be confident that the little we know of the things that cannot be otherwise is worthy of all our effort (*Ethics* 1177b31–78a2). We seem to be made for more than we are. Indeed, in a phrase from Saint Thomas' *De caritate* that E. F. Schumacher was fond of quoting, we read, "*Homo non est proprie humanus sed superhumanus est*" (Man is not properly human, but superhuman).[1] This is a theme to which the topic of

[1] "Man is properly not natural but supernatural." E. F. Schumacher, *A Guide for the Perplexed* (New York: Harper Colophon, 1977), 38.

order will often return us. Plato's Socrates, who did not much like imitations of any sort, notices, in the wonderful passage that introduces this chapter, that we are prone to "keep company" with the things that we admire. This ordinary observation means that we should pay particular attention to what are the things that we do in fact admire, as well as to the things we do not. Are the things that "accompany us" in fact themselves "orderly and divine"? And if so, what would this order entail?

Thus, if we keep company with "divine and orderly things", there is some chance that we should likewise reflect this company in our souls, in our lives, in our families, in our cities. We become what we love. And to love is always to choose, though to choose is not always to love rightly. This ordination to the higher things is not a hopeless endeavor, as Machiavelli, for one, suggested that it was. In his view, we should instead lower our sights to deal only with finite and fallible—indeed, corrupt—things. Our company, in his view, is to be less than divine and less than orderly. By not striving for the higher things, he thought, we could be given the lower things in relative comfort, or at least, in relative efficiency.

By contrast, I have always particularly liked the practical common sense of an Aristotle, a Samuel Johnson, a G. K. Chesterton in these matters. "We must not think that the man who is to be happy will need many things or great things, merely because he cannot be supremely happy without external goods", Aristotle told us. "For self-sufficiency and action do not involve excess, and we can do noble acts without ruling earth and sea; for even with moderate advantages one can act virtuously" (*Ethics* 1179a16). This passage is the great defense of the common man not merely in his daily affairs but in his own personal orientation to what is beyond himself. And if we can act virtuously at all, we already find ourselves subsequently oriented to things of truth that are, as it were, beyond virtue, wherein we begin to wonder about the whole order of things: How is it? Why is it? What is it for? How do I stand within it?

III

At the beginning of this book, on pages 5 and 6, are found five citations: one from Plato, one from Belloc, one from Aquinas, one from Pieper, and one from C. S. Lewis. Plato warns us that we can begin philosophy when we are too young to appreciate what it means to know things and to know that we know them. He recognizes that, properly speaking, knowing includes knowing the arguments by which the truth of things is established. But if we see everything controverted, if learned and famous men hold the opposite views on any given topic, it will naturally seem, especially if we are young, that it is impossible to sort things out. Cicero, in a famous comment cited approvingly by Pascal, Hobbes, and Descartes, remarked: "*Nihil tam absurde dici potest quod non dicatur ab aliquo philosophorum*" (Nothing can be stated that is so absurd that one of the philosophers will not affirm it). So philosophy is slandered. Relativism reigns supreme. Why make the effort if all we can hope for is an endless series of opinions and controversies with no hope of resolution or judgment at any level?

Socrates' point here, however, was not a sceptical one. His famous affirmation that he "knows little or nothing" is not spoken against what he does know. He simply admits that there is ever more to be known even of what he does already know. Socrates wanted to remind us that to know the truth of things, in their order, we have to be prepared to know what it is to know them. Too, following Aristotle, we have to have souls ready to seek the highest things even if they be found in ordinary circumstances. The highest things often have "footprints", as the medievals put it, among the lower things. Nothing is fully explained without everything, but what we do not yet know is not to be an excuse for not knowing what we can know.

The second passage at the beginning of this book is from a wonderful essay of Hilaire Belloc entitled "The Harbour in the North". I frankly consider Belloc to be the finest short essayist in the English language. This particular essay is among his most memorable ones. The essence of the story is that Belloc has sailed into a small port in northeast Scotland. It is early morning, before the sun is up. As he gets to the dock, he notices another boat there, on which he sees a man preparing to sail away. The man tells Belloc that he is on a mission to sail north to some mystical port. He is to sail by himself. This voyage of the unknown sailor symbolizes, of course, all of our searchings in all that we do. The man is to sail to a place where everything we know is forgotten, except those things that intimate to us that they "have their origins in joy". It is worth our lifetime, of course, to find what these things that cause us the final joy are about.

If we ask just what things do not have their "origins in joy", we can list only those things that do not originate in being, in *what is*—those things which, in that sense, lack being. This rootedness in joy, of course, brings us to the traditional definition of evil as precisely the lack of a good that ought to be in some being or action that in itself is good. This consequence raises the further question of whether there is an order in disorder, the declination of things from the good, of which Plato spoke in books 8 and

9 of the *Republic*. This is a question to which we will return in chapter 7. Evil fascinates us too much not to think about it.

IV

Thomas Aquinas, recalling Aristotle, said in a famous passage that "it is the nature of a wise man to order things" (*Sapientis est ordinare*). He then suggests that we can find a twofold order in things: first, that of the relation of the parts of something to each other so that they form a complete whole, and second, the order of the whole to some end or purpose beyond itself. Thus, we can say that a bicycle needs pedals, two wheels, a gear and chain mechanism, handlebars, and a frame. If all these parts are just lying about haphazardly on the ground, they do not form a bicycle. We cannot ride them in that chaotic state.

But once these parts are properly put together, the contraption just sits there until someone chooses to ride on it. This riding on it, peddling to some place on a man-propelled, two-wheeled conveyance, is what a bicycle is. The parts are ordered to each other so that the whole may do what it is supposed to do. We are to ride someplace by human power on this machine, but for our own purposes. The bicycle does not know where it is going. The bicycle is a tool or instrument that enables us to achieve our own good—or bad—purposes in a specific way. The universe itself, Aquinas thinks, has both its own internal order of parts to each other and an order of the whole to some purpose that explains its unity.

Aquinas next gives a broad overview to all of finite reality. He remarks that there is here a fourfold order that we can detect. The first order is that of the world itself. Its order we do not ourselves make or produce in the way it is found. We stand to this order as receivers and discoverers of what is already there. We may have to work and investigate to find the exact particulars of this order and the relation of things to one another. The order does not simply come out of our mind or imagination with no prior investigation of things. We are bound by what we find. But there is no doubt that our minds, in some basic sense, are curious to know how things fit together, their relationship to us and ours to them. Since we do not make this order to be what it is, we are recipient to its intelligibility.

We also note that the order of the cosmos does not understand itself as ordered or even as existing. It is not a single living being, as it were, with its own self-reflective intelligence. Within this same universe, we are the ones with the intelligence. We look at the cosmos; it does not look at us, unless there be an intelligent mind, as Socrates learned from Anaxagoras, that is the reason why things are what they are and act as they do (*Phaedo* 97c). The age-old question of whether something comes from nothing, of whether the cosmos is a chaos, or whether order can come from disorder, arises at this point.

On knowing what precisely "nothing" means, trying to elicit "something from nothing" is one of the great philosophic exercises that begin philosophy, and indeed grounds it. It is something that each mind must try to examine itself, so that it too will know the impossibility of something coming from nothing. If we really can, however, manage to convince ourselves that something comes from nothing, we live with something that cannot really be conceived. We deny the evidence of our minds themselves.

The next order is that of the mind itself, of logic, of the mind's relation of its own concepts to each other, of contraries and contradictories, of genus and species, of universals and particulars. It turns out that our minds have somehow their own rules or laws of operation that are part of their givenness as minds. Mind does not make itself to be mind. It discovers itself to be already mind. Logic is a tool or an art that guides our thinking. It is not thinking itself, but logic's rules, when correctly understood, are absolute.

The rules are also, in a sense, empty of content. Thus, I could say, "All turtles are green. Socrates is a turtle. Therefore, Socrates is green." In strict logic, aside from the truth of the propositions, which depends on our experience of the world, this is a valid argument or syllogism, as it is called, as to its form. Many philosophers from Abelard to Marx have confused the logical and the real orders, the conditions of humanity as a double abstraction with the conditions of particular men. This confusion is what gives poignancy to those quips often made of people like Rousseau who were said to have loved humanity but cared not much for Joseph and Sarah.

Let us suppose, however, that we argue, "Most men are liars. George is a man. Therefore, George is a liar." Looking at this proposition just as a proposition, knowing nothing about George's propensities, we can say without hesitation that this is not a valid argument, even if George is in fact a liar. We cannot accuse George on this basis alone. If George in fact is a liar, as he may well be, we need another argument or evidence to prove it. Thus, the rules of thought, while not substitutes for judgment and experience, can protect us from certain errors and assure us that certain arguments are valid. Knowing the order of mind, in this sense, is an aid to knowing for certain the truth of things.

The third order that Aquinas speaks of is the order in our actions. We refer here to the order of our voluntary actions, which can always be otherwise up to the point of our putting them into effect. To be "otherwise" simply means that some action other than the one we actually performed was in fact possible to us. Thus the proposition "If Socrates is sitting down in fact, it is eternally true that he was sitting down" is a true proposition and cannot be otherwise. But this *ex post facto* situation of Socrates sitting down when he is sitting down does not mean that his sitting down was determined or necessary before he accomplished his act, such that he had no other alternative before him.

Nor does this having sat down mean that Socrates cannot get up again and walk around if he so chooses. We arrive here at the realm of contingency, or possibility, in which lie ethics and politics. The world is full of things of creation or nature, things that, if they are there, are not there as a result of an act of the human will. On the other hand, the world also contains a realm of actions that were put into effect by solely human choices and subsequent acts. What exactly these actions are, how they come to be, their form, and their reality are the purpose of ethics and politics to describe and guide.

The final order in the world has to do with things that human beings make by art, craft, technology, or rhetoric (an inventive argument). Aristotle says that man is a being with a mind and a hand. The only way ideas or concepts that we conceive or devise can get out of our minds and into the world is for us to carry through what we think by fashioning some material thing outside of ourselves, outside of our mind. Our hands are the most obvious instruments of this endeavor. If I do not know what a chair is, for instance, I cannot make one except accidentally. But if

I know what one is, I still may not be able to make one, or certainly not a good one, unless I have the habit of art or craft by which I am able to guide my thought and hands in making exactly what I want.

This making is, along with ethics and politics, the function of "practical intellect", the use of the same intellect not simply to know (theoretical intellect), but to make or to do. If I accomplish what I want, the end product, the chair, looks pretty much as I first conceived it to be. It may even be better than I conceive it to be as I work at bringing the chair into existence. Art and craft presuppose that there is a world on which I can, and indeed should, impress my mind. They also presuppose beings with minds and hands.

Rhetoric, the art of persuasion, is the guidance of my words or speech such that I can convince someone to do something or to accept the validity of my argument. Persuasion is to be preferred to force, even though force may sometimes in reason still be necessary. Normally, human affairs should be accomplished by persuasion or oratory when it comes to affairs of right living in ethical and political life. Rhetoric, eloquence, and oratory are primarily arts, things that must be learned in order to be used well. Like all arts, they can be used badly; that is, oratory can be used well for a bad purpose, but in itself, it is a worthy habit and talent to acquire.

V

The fourth citation (on page 6) is from Josef Pieper, a man of extraordinary clarity. True philosophy does not exclude anything from its ken. This is not a statement without a history. It goes back to the difference between Aristotle and

Saint Thomas. Or perhaps, better, it goes back to the consequences of the difference between Aristotle and Aquinas in regard to the material available for them to know and with which they could work during their respective lifetimes. Something new existed in the time of Aquinas that did not exist in the time of Aristotle, something we call revelation. We can say of Aristotle, as Aquinas did, that he was "the Philosopher". Aristotle thought about what the human mind by itself could know, a noble enterprise. Few if any have done this better than Aristotle. Aquinas was careful to let Aristotle be Aristotle. But Aquinas began from revelation, from, to put it crudely, information unavailable to the natural human mind, but not information about which the human mind could not think once it knew what was presented to it.

Aristotle did not know revelation, either Jewish or Christian; therefore, it is sometimes claimed that his philosophy was "closed" to revelation. This latter conclusion is not that of Aquinas, though it is the conclusion of many thinkers about Aristotle who often end up suggesting that Aristotle would have rejected revelation on the grounds of philosophic integrity. Aquinas did not think that what Aristotle did not know made it impossible for him, on his own principles, to have considered some new information, wherever it came from. Aristotle's philosophic mind would have been open to confront what revelation might claim for itself.

What Aquinas did show, to make this point, was that, even while Aristotle did come to positions that are contrary to revelation—say, on the question of the eternity of the cosmos—on philosophic grounds, there was an argument for Aristotle's view that did not contradict reason. It would be possible, Aquinas argued, for an infinite Creator to create a finite cosmos from eternity. That God did not do so is a question of fact, known from revelation. But it was not impossible in logic or reason. Aristotle's philosophy was itself one that asked the proper questions and provided for principles that would allow revelational answers as answers precisely to legitimate philosophic questions, which it was the proper task of philosophy to formulate.

Pieper continues with the very Platonic and Augustinian point that "our longing for knowledge is beyond our control." We simply want to know. To know delights us. Plato called the philosopher the "lover" of wisdom as if to emphasize that we do not seek to know in some dispassionate sense. We have a genuine philosophic *eros*. Knowledge excites us, drives us. We speak of philosophers being "beside themselves" on discovering something or understanding something.

We are moved by "the wonder of the world"—that is, we wonder at the world, how it is, that it is, why it is. Plato speaks of this philosophic *eros* to remind us that seeking the truth of things is no indifferent activity of our souls. Pieper here describes something that we seek to recognize in this book. We are beings who want to know—and to know the truth. Even when we refuse some truth, as we can and sometimes do, we still do so in the name of truth. But we are made to be such beings that our very unknowing challenges us, unsettles us so that we seek to know the *what is* of everything we encounter, including ourselves.

VI

The final citation, found on page 6, from C. S. Lewis. I have often cited a passage from Lewis that simply said, "If you have only read a great book once, you have not read it at all." I have noted that there are some books that we can read every year and find them to be new books each time or contain riches that we never previously noticed. I have known men who read Tolkien every year. This urge to reread surprises us, but it is true that we can do it, and we want to do it. It is also obvious that we cannot read a great book twice if we have not read it once.

The teacher guides us through the first time. The reading that takes us through this first time is itself a seminal and often profound experience. Yet it is quite possible that we miss the import of a book on its first reading. We can read Aristotle or Augustine or Burke or Walker Percy and miss his whole point. But the opposite is true too. We can read them and be bowled over by them. Only lately, after I had read several books twenty or thirty times, did I come across the passage from Lewis in which he tells us that we, if we read great works, will do so many times, twenty or thirty in our lives.

It is said of the philosopher Eric Voegelin that he read the works of Shakespeare every year. Think of the enormous discipline this entailed, of the store of wisdom with which he refreshed himself each year. We know those who read the Bible regularly. We will learn much of what life is about from our own living, from our reflecting on what actually happens to us and those we love. But likewise, much that we know we must learn from others, from experiences that we shall never ourselves have but know only through what we read. Somehow the experience of others is not to be lost to us.

We live to know more than ourselves, even though "know thyself" remains our first duty. But what is present in both Pieper and Lewis is the notion that we delight in knowing. We often notice that when we begin a project or read a book, time passes unnoticed, almost as if we stand outside of time. We are moved to our core by what is to be wondered at. Everything *that is* we find not merely admirable, but something that incites us, something that makes us realize that the world is more than ourselves yet also includes us in some order we seek to clarify.

Aquinas has a peculiar question, "*utrum veritas sit specialis virtus*"—whether truth is a special virtue (II–II 109, 2). The question arises because the truth is primarily a question of the intellect, of both the intellectual and practical virtues. On the other hand, whether we act to tell the truth when the occasion arises indicates a moral attitude. Thus, the moral virtue of truth-telling means not only that we know the truth but that we speak it, attest to it. The good of man consists in using his mind properly.

Aquinas then cites Augustine, who said the good consists in "order". The special character of the good is the manifestation of a definite order. There is a special order in which our exterior words or acts are duly ordained to something, as a sign to that which is signified within us. And this is what perfects a man through order—that is, he manifests in his words and acts the order of a thing *that is*. The very good of his mind is to know and manifest this order.

VII

Let us, then, consider the various kinds of order that we might encounter. The mind wants to know that this thing is not that thing. It strives to distinguish. It seeks to know and manifest the differences among things, including human things. The human mind implicitly assumes there is order among things because it looks for it. We have to be talked out of order with very delicate arguments or proofs to think that there is no order or that the only order that exists is the one we impose on things.

The great Church Doctor Athanasius, in his *Discourse against the Pagans*, stated what is no doubt the common view.

> It is right that creation should exist as he made it and as we see it happening, because this is his will, which no one would deny. For if the movement of the universe were irrational, and the world rolled on in random fashion, one would be justified in disbelieving what we say. But if the world is founded on reason, wisdom and science, and is filled with orderly beauty, then it must owe its origin and order to none other than the Word of God.[2]

The order is a willed order. It is not irrational, though its rationality is not a manmade rationality. This origin does not mean that human minds cannot know something of it, beginning from *what is*. The world does not roll on in a random fashion.

The way to become divine and orderly is to "keep company with divine and orderly things", as Plato said. In the *Phaedo*, we again come across something that Socrates learned from Anaxagoras, in a book that he said could be purchased for a small cost at the local booksellers.

> I once heard someone reading from a book by Anaxagoras, and asserting that it is Mind that produces order and is the cause of everything. This explanation pleased me. Somehow it seemed right. Mind should be the cause of everything; and I reflected that if this is so, Mind in producing order sets everything in order and arranges each individual thing in the way that is best for it (97c).

[2] Athanasius, *Discourse against the Pagans* 40, in *The Liturgy of the Hours*, Thursday, First Week in Ordinary Time.

Such is the theme of this book: mind and order in the various levels of being, including the order within our own souls and our own polities. There remain, of course, those who find no order or reason in reality. They even, somewhat illogically perhaps, spend a good deal of time explaining why it is "reasonable" that there is no order or reason in things. The fact is that the mind is made, not by itself, to know *what is*, and as best it can, does so. We want to know, we have a longing to know, the "order of things". Let us see what we can make of the various orders within this general order, which, as Socrates said, is made to be ordered by Mind.

CHAPTER II

THE ORDER WITHIN THE GODHEAD

Yet, it is not without reason that in this Trinity only the Son is called the Word of God, and that only the Holy Spirit is the Gift of God, and that only He, of whom the Son was begotten, and from whom the Holy Spirit principally proceeds, is God the Father. I have added "principally", therefore, because the Holy Spirit is also found to proceed from the Son. But the Father also gave this to Him, not as though He already existed and did not yet have it, but whatever He gave to the only-begotten Word, he gave by begetting Him. He so begot Him, therefore, that the common Gift should also proceed from Him, and that the Holy Spirit should be the spirit of both.

—Augustine *On the Trinity*[1]

The Christian confession of faith in God as the Three-in-One, as he who is simultaneously the *monas* and the *trias*, absolute unity and fullness, signifies the conviction that divinity lies beyond our categories of unity and plurality. Although to us, the nondivine, it is one and single, the one and only divine as opposed to all that is not divine; nevertheless in itself it is truly fullness and plurality, so that creaturely unity

[1] Augustine *On the Trinity* 15.17, ed. Gareth B. Matthews and trans. Stephen McKenna (Cambridge: Cambridge University Press, 2002).

and plurality are both in the same degree a likeness and a share of the divine.

—Joseph Ratzinger[2]

I

The treatment of the inner life of God is not generally the first thing we deal with in considering the order of things, however important this inner life might be in itself, even to the order of things themselves not divine. Normally, in speculative things, we human beings begin with what is most familiar to us. We next carefully work our way, distinction by distinction, to the more difficult and abstruse subjects by making sure that our process is logical and factually correct. Indeed, the Trinity, as the inner life of God is technically called, is more likely to be the last thing considered, if it is treated at all. Yet it is the most exciting and basic of all topics, the one that really gets to the heart of things, of why things are and why things are as they are.

No doubt, if we have an idea of everything else, we will be in a better position to gain some insight into the trinitarian origin of things. This step-by-step process is certainly a legitimate procedural approach whose validity is not intended to be denied here. Nonetheless, beginning with the inner life of the Godhead has certain advantages. It allows us to see what is at stake from the very beginning: namely, that behind order is not chaos, but precisely a higher order—order upon order. The effort to understand

[2] Joseph Ratzinger [Benedict XVI], *Introduction to Christianity*, trans. J. R. Foster, 2nd ed. (San Francisco: Ignatius Press, 2004), 178.

what is handed down to us about the Godhead broadens our minds so that we can, insofar as possible to us, think what this inner life might mean, for we, as Joseph Ratzinger put it, have "a likeness and a share" in this life as our own perfection.

Many people, however, are content simply to call the Trinity a "mystery" or a "myth"—and then not think seriously about it at all. But "mystery" is not as such opposed to thought, nor is "myth" devoid of profound meaning, as we can see in the works of a Plato or a Tolkien. Thinking accurately about what God might be like is, perhaps, analogous to crossing an intellectual minefield unscathed.[3] Yet, if we are to know this reality, even in our own limited way, we sometimes must make the effort to cross this very minefield. Probably no subject is more fraught with potential errors than the Trinity, except perhaps the Incarnation, to which it is directly related. Indeed, it might be said that what we do know of the Trinity we owe to erroneous explanations of it together with the Church's historic efforts to correct and clarify them. It is in this sense that all heresy serves a useful intellectual purpose. Aquinas taught us to see such errors as ways to truth.

Still, in the tradition of Aristotle, it is worth the effort to know what we can about the highest things, however little it might be. The notion that a person cannot learn something from trinitarian discussions because he may not believe in the doctrine strikes me as a kind of agnosticism or closed-mindedness. It may indeed be rooted in a fear that thinking about the Trinity as such might just have something to do with reality, which, if true, we cannot avoid. But we can

[3] See James V. Schall, *What Is God Like?* (Staten Island, N.Y.: Alba House, 1992).

and should test what we do not believe, particularly when other authorities and thinkers hold that it is believable or thinkable. Few subjects concentrate the mind more directly on what our lives are about than that of the Trinity. The notion that we are persons related to others in our very being and knowing is itself a long-range result of our reflecting on what Father, Son, and Spirit might mean, on Word and Love as expressions of our relatedness to others and to *what is*.

Only Christianity, to be sure, has a doctrine of the self-sufficient inner life of God. Both Islam and Judaism, also monotheistic religions, with the latter at the origins of Christianity itself, specifically reject this notion of a vibrant inner life within God. Or, such an inner life, they do not accept that we can know it, or that it is accurately described as trinitarian. Christians themselves, of course, do not claim to know anything of this life by their own intellectual powers, or even much of it with all the insight they can muster based on the stimulus and gift of revelation. This relative lack of knowledge, however, is not conceived to be a lessening or denigration of the great powers of the human intellect. In fact, thinking about this divine inner life enlarges our intellectual scope. In considering the Trinity's very possibility and dynamics, it forces us to examine more closely what we know or can know even about created things.

Our intellects, while being actual powers of the soul, stand lowest, not highest, on the scale of intellectual beings, of which the Deity, however it is to be conceived, is the highest. We have minds to know the truth; we are not Truth itself. This is why, himself having a mind, as we saw in the preface, Socrates was struck by Anaxagoras' observation that the cosmos, in its order, revealed mind.

Some, like the Stoics, even want to make this cosmos a god, or like Hegel, a gradual manifestation of the Spirit's coming-to-be. But the Trinity points us in another, more fruitful, direction, one that does not make the world to be a god simply because it also reveals mind. The world did not give itself its own order or mind, even if it gives hints of both.

II

That there is an inner life of God is considered to be something that cannot be known by reason alone or known directly. We may find hints of it in both the Old Testament and in Greek or other philosophic thought, with their emphasis on wisdom, *logos*, goodness, and spirit. When Aristotle said that the First Mover moved by thought and love, he seems to have referred to things moved from the outside in response to the First Mover. But his thought was very close to the truth in another way. If the First Mover moves by thought and love, it stands to reason that it contains such realities within itself. Logically, however, if we knew the full inner life of God by our own powers, we would have to be God ourselves, which is not the case. That God could make Himself known to us in some fashion and that we have powers to understand this "having been made known" brings us close to a proper understanding of both metaphysics and revelation.

Few there are who, on self-reflection, are not aware of their own finiteness, of the fact that they did not cause their own existences to burst forth out of nothingness. No thing, certainly no human thing, caused itself to be what it is: this thing, not that thing. Those who are not aware of these limitations in themselves—or worse, those who do not grant them, once knowing them—are probably the most dangerous of our kind. Augustine links this latter view directly to the notion of pride, which locates any cause of being in ourselves. Thus, while recognizing the temptation, most human beings look with some bemusement on those of our species who claim divine powers for themselves or even for the race as a whole or for some part of it. Normally, this consideration that our finite intellectual powers do not know God's inner life would settle the case. What we cannot know does not seem to occupy much of our time, however curious about it we might be.

Christian revelation, whether we like it or not, however, exists in the world as an intelligible explication of things. Revelation proposes some account, some indication, of this inner life of the Godhead. The Trinity simply exists as one among the various explanations of *things that are*. It is intended to alert us to more than we might think possible to know by our own powers. It is also a response to things we do know. Furthermore, it proclaims this inner life to be consistent and coherent, both in itself and in relation to what is not God. We cannot merely ignore what this inner life might mean and still claim total intellectual integrity. We must seek to account for its feasibility, as it were.

When sorted out on its own grounds, this revelation finds that there is a diversity of what came to be called Persons within the Godhead, a diversity that, when carefully spelled out, did not run against the unity of the same Godhead. This diversity is described, as we see in Athanasius and Augustine, in terms of three Persons. All three Persons are variously described in Scripture as agents in the mission of Christ in the world. Indeed, Christ Himself, as a Person, is understood accurately only when He is seen as an equal participant of this inner life within the Godhead, true God as well as true man.

Scripture does not contain, as it were, an independent dissertation on each Person apart from His function or operation with regard to Christ's mission in this world and hence to us human beings. The main burden of this mission is to point out the final and proper end for which each human being was created in the first place and the relation of all else to this purpose. It also provides a scheme or means by which this purpose is to be achieved by those to whom it is addressed. But that there is a diversity of Persons and a unity in the same Godhead remains evident throughout careful reading of the sources.

This lack of a direct or separate treatment of each Person, nonetheless, is not intended to prevent us from knowing what we can of this inner life on the basis of what we have been told or what is handed down. Efforts further to clarify what each Person is are aided both by what we know of the other divine Persons and from philosophy confronted with reality. Since creation is conceived to be the product of all three Persons, it is rightly suspected that something of this inner life will be reflected in what we know of the world and of one another—of ourselves even, as Augustine will show, particularly in our own knowing and willing powers.

We constantly are confronted by things that, by being and remaining themselves, relate to something else. We know about common goods that include and presuppose the particular good, as if otherness and diversity are also intrinsic to being, without being at the same time not-being. But there always must be a unity that explains why the parts are the parts. We do not know what "parts" are, in fact, if we do not know how they are related to the whole of which they are parts. We do not know what our hand is, for example, unless we know it as related to and belonging to our own types of bodies. No one thing, in fact, that we encounter is known in total isolation from other things, even when we consider it, as we can, in isolation from other things.

Scripture itself thus does not directly address this topic of the inner life of the Godhead. Neither Paul nor the evangelists make a big issue of it, even though everything needed for its spelling out is found in these sources. What Scripture presents, rather, is an account of creation, of the Incarnation and Redemption of Christ, and of their context and purpose. But in the process of explaining who Christ is and what He is about, we find texts that relate Him to His Father, or to the Holy Spirit, or to both. He says He is one with the Father and that He will send the Holy Spirit. No one knows the Father but the Son, and no one knows the Son but the Father. We are told to baptize in the name of the Father, the Son, and the Holy Spirit. Why not just in the name of God? Because the name of God is, in fact, Father, Son, and Holy Spirit. That is the point. That is what is given to us to ponder.

Needless to say, the human mind, out of simple curiosity or wonder, wants to know something more about this inner life than merely its existence or the names of the participants, as it were. Do the names themselves of these three Persons have any significance? Could they have other names? Does it make any difference that God is called "Father" and not "Mother" or "Henry" or "It"? It is normal, Aquinas thought, that when we know of the existence or activity of something, we want to know more completely in what consists the full existence and being of what causes our curiosity. We want to have this information more fully perhaps because it might be useful to us, but primarily because we would just like to know. The highest levels of our thinking seem to be concerned primarily with things we just want to know about, as if they are more fascinating than those things that might fall under our own creative powers and about which we can more easily gain adequate information.

It is not without importance that Aquinas, in discussing what ultimately constitutes our happiness, does not hesitate to say that it is a "beatific vision" when we know precisely what this God wants us to know of His inner life. We are to see Him "face to face", as Saint Paul emphasizes. But again, even when we know Him face to face, we want to remain what we are—human beings, not turtles, not gods. Indeed, this "vision", while it requires additional grace, seems to be the purpose for our entire existence in the first place. Somehow, what we are, the very structure of our being, is bound up with this inner life of the Godhead. We are not necessary to it, no doubt. We need not exist for God's completion or happiness. But the very way we are in existence is designed so that we can potentially, at least, receive what is beyond our natural capacities, themselves not of our own making either.

III

The word "Trinity" does not itself appear in Scripture. This lack does not mean that it is some sort of aberration, however. It is a useful word to describe accurately what Scripture tells us about the inner life of God. If we use philosophic or newly coined terms carefully and know what we are talking about, there is nothing wrong with using them to describe truths found in Scripture. Scripture, however unique it is in many ways, does not mandate our using only scriptural terms to explain either it or ourselves. We can use non-scriptural words to identify what is said in revelation provided that we clearly know what our terms mean in describing or making intelligible what we find in Scripture.

Scripture, again, was not designed to forbid us from using terms that are not found in Scripture itself. Nor was it designed to prevent us from thinking about what we find there. Rather, the opposite is the case. Scripture was itself addressed to our intelligence. It cannot be understood without the intellectual effort to know what it is talking about. It is not for the intellectually slothful, nor does it shun subtle and penetrating ideas that require the deepest of our reflections. The purpose of revelation, however, is not obscurity, but clarity. The very wrestling with what Scripture might mean has the indirect result of bringing forth otherwise overlooked insights and principles in natural philosophy itself.

The Nicene Creed, finally formulated in its present form in A.D. 325, is the briefest and most authoritative summary of what the Christian faith holds about God. It is structured precisely after the sequence and meaning of the Persons of the Trinity. The word "Trinity" seems to have been first used by Theophilus of Antioch about A.D. 180 in its Greek form, *trias*; Tertullian uses the Latin form *Trinitas*. The first credal form is from Gregory Thaumaturgus about A.D. 270: "There is therefore nothing created, nothing subject to another in the Trinity; nor is there anything that has been added as though it once had not existence, but had entered afterwards; therefore the Father has never been without the Son, nor the Son without the

Spirit; and this same Trinity is immutable and unalterable forever."[4]

To be "immutable" and "unalterable", moreover, does not designate inertness or lack of inner dynamism, but the opposite. For something to be mutable or alterable would imply a lack, a deficiency, in it. In the case of the Trinity, it would mean that the inner life of God was itself incomplete and in need of something beyond itself. This would imply that God is not fully God since He needs something from outside of Himself. Almost all theories that reject the Trinity as the proper explanation of the inner life of the Godhead seek to prove that such a trinitarian explanation of God cannot hold. Trinitarian theories in their proper sense seek to establish that no greater idea or reality of God exists but the one found in the trinitarian explanation.

Thus, if we are to lead "orderly and divine" lives, as Plato tells us that we should, it seems that they will have, as a principle of our own inner order, some relation to the inner life of the Godhead, whatever it might be. Theologians and philosophers have been pondering this inner life of God for centuries, first under the aspect of how this life relates to Christ of Nazareth and ultimately under the effort to grasp what it is in itself insofar as we can comprehend it. But the assumption seems reasonable enough that the order of stable

[4] G. H. Joyce, "The Blessed Trinity", in *The Catholic Encyclopedia* (New York: Encyclopedia Press, 1913–1922), online at www.newadvent.org/cathen/15047a.htm. See also Ratzinger, *Introduction to Christianity*, 2nd ed., 162–90; See James V. Schall, "The Trinity: God Is Not Alone", in *Redeeming the Time* (New York: Sheed & Ward, 1968), 65–96; "Trinitarian Transcendence in Ignatian Spirituality", in *The Distinctiveness of Christianity* (San Francisco: Ignatius Press, 1982), 114–25; and "The Trinity: 'So Aweful a Subject in Mixed Company'", in *What Is God Like?* (Collegeville, Minn.: Michael Glazer / Liturgical Press, 1992), 171–91.

relationships within the Godhead is at the origin of what the world and our lives are about. This order is what lies behind all other order. What proceeds from this inner life of God will not be totally unreflective of the inner dynamism of what is not God, whatever it be. Yet what remains finite can only reflect, in a finite way, what is not finite. We remain inside of the world looking at its order, even when we know and cause our own disorder. And, to repeat, we cannot know disorder without knowing some order. Accounting for disorder is the other side of accounting for order.

To the classical writers—Aristotle, for instance—the First Mover, or God, did not seem to care for anything outside of itself. Moreover, this Mover was apparently lonely—that is, it seemed to be isolated in its grandeur and separateness. The First Mover moved others, as we mentioned, by their "love and thought" about it. But it seemed rather inert, though love and thought are signs of inner activity. Still, these very deficiencies in the philosophic Godhead appeared to be unusually fruitful when thought about. Perhaps more was to be known if we set about learning of this inner life properly. This suspicion proves especially insightful when the revelation of the inner life of God is seen in relation to what we can know of God by reason alone.

Philosophy and revelation both claim to explain, or seek to explain, the essentials of the whole. What if God was not lonely; what if He did not need creation or others at all? What, in other words, if His inner life was "personal", related to Persons, yet complete within itself? This alternative certainly would put a new slant on the supposed deficiencies in the Godhead. The very natural "deficiencies"—loneliness, no concern for what is not God—seemed to find responses in the revelational descriptions of the inner life of God. Could this be merely accidental?

Frank Sheed, a famed speaker and debater in London, used to say that, judged by audience reactions, the Trinity was by far the most fascinating topic that he ever lectured on. He said that it was always the one topic to which people listened carefully, in stillness. It had a certain fascination that was unexpected, and even inexplicable, almost as if people realized that ultimate things were being discussed. These were things everyone has, at some time or another, wondered about. In this chapter, what I mean by "the Trinity" is the basic doctrine that is taught by the Church over the centuries, which is defined or discussed in the teaching documents of the Church. I will not go into a long and detailed scriptural account of how this doctrine appears there or of the principal theological controversies in which the central definitions were hammered out.

This spelling out of what the Trinity means has been accomplished in numerous places and often. (The latest is in the *Catechism of the Catholic Church*.) Frank Sheed's discussion of the Trinity, in fact, remains one of the best.[5] I am not directly interested here in the heresies, those explanations that would not accept the full force of the teaching that within the Godhead are three equal yet different divine Persons, but one God. What is most astonishing is not the heretical explications of the Trinity, but the orthodox explanation. No doubt, as we indicated, it was the debates with the heretics that occasioned the more precise understanding of the Trinity to come about, but these debates are by now well known. Error itself serves the orderly function of making truth more precise.

[5] Frank Sheed, *Theology and Sanity* (San Francisco: Ignatius Press, 1993), 88–115.

IV

In George W. Bush's second inaugural address (2005), he stressed the importance of individual liberty, self-reliance, private ownership of property, and initiative. Then, almost as if to counteract any sense of isolation or closed autonomy that this individualist emphasis might imply, he added, "In America's ideal of freedom the exercise of rights is ennobled by service and mercy, and a heart for the weak. Liberty for all does not mean independence from one another. Our nation relies on men and women who look after a neighbor and surround the lost with love."

Behind these traditional and noble notions of a sense of individual dignity and independence—"We have proclaimed that every man and woman on this earth has rights and dignity and matchless value because they bear the image of the maker of heaven and earth"—are an equally strong sense of service and outwardness to others. There is here an implicit unity and plurality that is already present in the culture. Richness and liberty are not for themselves alone. Liberty is not independence from one another, but a relatedness to one another. The juxtaposing of these ideas is not accidental but the residue of long traditions on the nature of the life of God as it is manifested in the Trinity, in oneness and otherness, and reflected in the cosmos and in human life.[6]

Just before reading this inaugural address, I had heard an explanation for the delay in Muslim aid for the victims of the 2004 tidal wave in South Asia. This delay seemed strange

[6] Benedict XVI's encyclical *Deus Caritas Est* (San Francisco: Ignatius Press, 2006), explicitly goes into the relation of love to service to others, the relation of both to government and the Church, and their orderly place in our lives.

because most of those suffering were Muslims. The answer was that, in Muslim theology, all things are viewed as the direct result of God's will, with no provision for secondary causes; therefore, natural disasters are considered to be acts of Allah punishing those who are not living according the Koranic law. Therefore, if God is punishing those people through natural disasters, it seems nothing less than blasphemous to help them.

What do we make of this latter theory? In a way, it goes back to the New Testament itself, where Christ was asked whether the tower falling on passersby and killing them was in punishment for their sins. Significantly, He said no. The supposition found in the President's address is that we are responsible for helping in natural disasters, a Christian supposition. It is clear, in any case, that our actions are ultimately shaped by what we understand the Godhead, or its equivalent in our own philosophy, to be like.

It is not merely believers whose actions are shaped by their theology or world view. "By their fruits you shall know them" applies equally to believers and nonbelievers, to adherents of any or to no theological or philosophic position. Moreover, a philosophic or theological system has to account not only for what happens when its followers observe its tenets, but likewise for what happens when they do not. In this sense, Christianity is as much a theory of what happens when believers sin as of what happens when they do not. And a theory that claims that Christians either do not or cannot sin is not a Christian theory, for the very basis of Christianity is the forgiveness of sins, not the total eradication of sinners in this world.

Chesterton said that religions are really pretty much alike when it comes to their external practices and garb. Where they differ radically is over what they understand God, themselves, and the world to be like. George Cardinal Pell of

Sydney made the same point in another way. "The story of the Fall, the doctrine of original sin which explains the presence of evil in the world (an evil presence which God does not want), not only separates Christianity from religions of the East such as Hinduism, but also from many contemporary pagans who deny the existence of evil in men's hearts and place it somewhere else, outside in the structures of society."[7]

If we think the cause of evil does not ultimately lie in ourselves, in some voluntary disorder, but in political or cosmic forces outside of ourselves, we cannot but end in denying that God is good if He is indeed the Creator of this same universe in which we live and in which we find the disorder known as "evil" or "sin". But the point I wish to emphasize is that an aberrant view about the origin of evil—say, the ancient Manichean view that there is a God of evil—necessitates logically an understanding of God's very being that places Him in an adversarial relation to our own presumed good. Though we will go into this question of the order of evil later (chapter 7), it is enough to note that rejecting one understanding of God always lands us in a contrary one. We do not escape the "God problem", that is, our effort to explain things, by disbelief in any particular understanding of God. We merely locate our explanation someplace else, even if we call it atheism.

V

The Christian view that there is one God in whom are three distinct, divine Persons will strike us as paradoxical or

[7] George Cardinal Pell, *Be Not Afraid: Collected Writings* (Sydney: Duffy & Snellgrove, 2000), 69.

contradictory if we do not carefully think about it. Basically, the Christian view begins from the notion that God does not need anything else but Himself. Particularly, He does not need what we call creation—that which we first experience and somehow want to call necessary. His inner order is, as such, complete, needing nothing further. But if this position is valid, it must confront the question of perfections outside the Godhead that seem to indicate the danger or falsity of this view of the Godhead as complete in itself.

At the human level, Aristotle asked the question of whether we could or would call someone happy who had everything that would be needed or even conceivable for a happy life—riches, knowledge, virtue—but who, at the same time, lacked friends. To this question, Aristotle answered, wisely, that no one would call such a person happy who had all else but lacked friends. It seems obvious, as Aristotle brilliantly explains, that having friends is a good and a perfection of being, the lack of which would subvert the very notion of happiness.

If we can extrapolate from this view about the self-sufficiency of God, it would seem that any intelligent being who is simply by itself would be lonely or insufficient. It would lack that against which it might see or know or love even itself. We see no reason why this thinking, this perfection of friends, does not apply to the Godhead on an even more exalted scale. A god who thus lacked friends, however conceived, would seem to be an incomplete being. This is a puzzle, no doubt. Either we have to explain why a god without friends is better than one with them, or else we have to explain that there is something in the Godhead that corresponds with the essence of what we mean by friendship. Monotheistic notions of God seem to accept that

God is exalted over friendship since He exists or lives in isolation. The fact is that this position heightens the distance between God and man. In some sense, it even seems to make finite life superior to the transcendent life of God. A perfection was put into the world that had no analogous origin in the Godhead.

Christianity, of course, does conceive God to be unique, one. Moreover, it accepts Aristotle's view that friendship in or with God would seem itself to necessitate something divine, something on the same level. That is, a divine friendship would not be complete if the beings involved in this relationship were themselves less than gods—human beings, for instance. This conclusion leaves the question of whether God and man can be friends as its own poignant problem. Clearly this issue is addressed by the Incarnation: in John's Gospel, we are specifically told that we are to be called God's friends.

But here the problem is within the Godhead itself. The parameters of the discussion are defined by the need to preserve the unity of the Godhead and to find an alterity that would make otherness possible and intelligible. This question is also somewhat related to Aristotle's wonderment about how many good friends we could have. He did not think it was possible to have more than one or a few. The doctrine of the Trinity seems to reflect this view in a kind of transcendent manner. And at the human level, it implies that the highest relation we can have with even other human beings is itself limited to a few. Our problem is time. We do not have enough time to know more than a few well. This fact makes us wonder if there is not something beyond time—eternity.

One solution to the problem of divine friendship might be that there are two or more gods, the polytheistic position. Just as kings can be said to be friends only with other kings, so God could be a friend only of other gods. But this hypothesis would imply either a group of lesser gods, each of whom has a distinct purpose, so that one could be distinguished from the other, or it supposes two perfect gods who have no distinction one from another, since both are equally perfect. All pagan and polytheistic religions have explored the problem of the varied activities of the multiplicity of gods.

Plato is famous for being scandalized at the undisciplined and often unedifying activities of the gods of Olympus. This critique of the pagan gods set him on the intellectual journey to find the Good that was not subject to the foibles of the many gods, to Socrates' "spirit". Indeed, we might argue that philosophy itself was invented to replace the quarreling gods precisely because of the difficulty in distinguishing the multiplicity of the gods. Plato was very much in search of what did not deviate from the Good.

But if two "perfect" gods are a contradiction, we are left with one God, who is indeed good and therefore not like other gods. Can we conceive, then, a single God in whom the problems that we are concerned about, that of sameness and otherness, that of loneliness, can be resolved? Is there an order of understanding that could provide a plausible grasp of God that would save the uniqueness of the one God while, at the same time, addressing the problem of loneliness or otherness in God?

The raw material we have to work on, no doubt, is provided for us in the revelation of the Trinity. It seems perfectly clear that this doctrine or understanding suggests both unity and otherness within the Godhead, as if to say that God *is*, but is not lonely. And the reason that God is not lonely is that the very meaning of the Trinity relates to the question of otherness in God. The fullness of life in the

Godhead is a personal relationship. Indeed, the very notion of "person" in our tradition, even with its origin in Greek drama, is due to theological efforts to understand the differences within the Godhead.

To the question of how we could address the problem of a single God within whom there is still diversity, we have the reflections of Augustine, who devoted a good deal of attention to this very issue. Augustine, of course, is not unrelated to Plato. Like Plato, he wanted to know the proper location of the "Republic". Plato found that it was in speech or mind, where it could exist secure apart from the varieties of actual regimes. Augustine, in his *City of God*, goes beyond this Platonic view, worthy as it is. Augustine shows that our own happiness cannot be properly located anyplace else but in contemplation and love of the inner life of God, should it be offered to us. In this sense, Augustine relativizes all the alternative descriptions of the actual content of ultimate human happiness. He did not do this by denying the good that is found in *what is*, but by indicating that all good points to that Good that is the locus of ultimate order in all things. That location is the inner life of the Trinity.

Augustine addressed himself to the following question: Can there be an otherness within something that does not destroy the unity of a thing? To answer this question, he turned to our powers of knowing and willing. We are, we know, and we will, but in performing these acts, we are one. It is I who am, I who know, and I who will. Augustine found that the very nature of knowledge implied that the being that knows becomes, in knowing, something other than its bare existence. But this new knowing does not mean that what knows becomes two or more separate beings. It remains itself. Thus, Christ was described as the "Word" of the Father.

This designation indicated to Augustine the possibility that within the Godhead there could be a diversity that encompassed the wholeness of God. While remaining God, the Word was totally related to the divine origin, the Father. The Word was the Word of the Father, nothing else.

The Persons in the Godhead, the Father, the Son, and the Spirit, are not three separate substances or subsistent beings, as is often claimed. My knowledge of something else, on reflection, does not make me two persons, but one person related to something else that is known by me. Philosophers came to designate the Persons in the Godhead as falling in the category of relation, not substance. This understanding meant that the whole being of the Father, the Son, and the Spirit is related to one another within the same being. Their diversity of origin, begetting, and procession remains without creating three separate beings, but still one is not the other's uniqueness.

What this unity in diversity implies is that the very notion of "person" cannot be what it is unless it is open toward, related to, something else for its complete reality. Or better, its complete reality is to be related to another. This is ultimately why all philosophy of person will emphasize this openness to others. God is not completely understood as Father *or* Son *or* Spirit, but as Father *and* Son *and* Spirit. This is what the vital inner life of God includes of its very nature. Its very otherness implies a completeness within itself.

VI

So, what follows from this understanding that within the inner life of the Godhead there is a diversity of Persons such that God is in fact lacking of no perfection, such as friendship? Initially, it means that what is not God, what is outside of God, if it exists in fact, is not the product of necessity. That is to say, what is not God need not exist. God would be perfect and complete even if there were nothing besides God. The universe plus God does not make God "more" than He is. The existence of the finite world does not complete the existence of the infinite God, as if God were lacking something.

Of course, we inquire into this question while being perfectly aware, in spite of the fact that we have minds, that we are not gods. That is to say, something that is not God does in fact exist. If something besides God does exist, however, it cannot be claimed that it caused its own existence or that it came into being apart from God's origin of all order in being. Finite existence, as Aquinas tells us, still must be traced to God as its source and cause of what it is *to be*.

What is that exists but not of necessity must find its origin in something other than its own being. Aquinas remarked that the world is created in mercy, not in justice. If the world were created in justice, because of something owed to it, it would evidently follow that God was somehow necessitated to create. This is but another version of the same problem of seeing God as a necessary creator of what is not God. When we locate the origin of things in mercy or love rather than in justice, we take a momentous step. We know that God Himself, in the relations of His inner life, is necessarily what He is. His life cannot be other than it is; it already contains all being and good. But this perfection implies not a lack, but a fullness. God is perfectly God even if nothing besides God exists.

This alternative means that what is not God must be a result of something in God that is beyond justice or necessity. What might this alternative be? The fullness or abundance of the divine life does not necessitate that something other than God exists. Nor, by this same fullness, is God, should He will, prohibited from causing what is not Himself to exist. If God did not need to cause something that is not Himself to exist, nonetheless, by the same token, He is free to cause something not Himself to be. He is, in other words, free with regard to the existence or nonexistence of what is not Himself. But if God freely causes what is not Himself to exist, we can, on the basis of His own merciful purpose in creation, anticipate or expect that His loyalty or fidelity will be freely given to what He causes to be.

If we return to the inner life or order within the Godhead, we see that the love of the Father and the Son is understood to be Gift, to be Spirit, to be what God is after the manner of receiving *what is* as both existence and Word. In Plato's *Symposium* there is a discussion of whether the world is complete if there is within it no principle of return, no appreciation of what causes reality. Being seems to require reflection of itself, affirmation of its own goodness. It is along these lines that trinitarian thought tends when it says that the entire Trinity creates and that its internal order ends in Gift and Mission, of being received and of being capable of being imitated. And once created, it seems that creation needs and has the capacity to respond to its own cause in the manner in which its existence was originally given, that is, out of love or mercy, not necessity.

We arrive at a position, then, that suggests that if anything but God exists, it exists not because God is lonely within His internal life such that He needed something else besides Himself to be complete. Since God is not lonely, but rather has the ultimate diversity of perfect Persons within His own divine being, it follows that what is not God will, in its own way, manifest the non-loneliness or friendship that is characteristic of the inner life of God. The first point of what is not God will be the last point, as it were, of what is within God. And the last point of the inner life of God is the receptivity in which the love of the Father and Son is reflected in the Person of the Spirit as an all-consuming love. What bursts forth from God will do so at this point. This is why the Spirit is conceived after the manner of Gift, of something that is a sign of what is beyond necessity, of the wonder of what is totally received, both being and life.

But love is always love of something. Since all things are created in the Word, in the full understanding of the Father that is the Son, what is not God is intelligible as a possible reflection of something that God is. In this sense, God would know the world and what is in it even if the world did not exist. When God creates the world, thinking in our own terms, the world is not a surprise to Him, revealing to Him something about which He had no previous idea.

But the order of the world, as it were, does not start with the whole world, but with those creatures who are most like God, that is, those with intelligences and wills. These creatures are logically before the rest of creation, at least in intention. This means that the highest point of contact between the inner life of God and the life of the world is at the point where an intelligent creature is capable of receiving a gift and returning it to its source. In this sense, the human person precedes in intention the world itself such that the order of the world is related to the inner order of the human soul and that to which it is itself ordained.

Since the inner life of the Godhead is Trinity, a Trinity of Persons, we can expect that what is not God will be ordered to persons who stand in relation to what is other than themselves. The high point of what is not God is what is most like unto God in creation. And what is most like unto God will be something that can manifest what is most exalted within the Godhead, namely, the free relation of person to person. When Augustine in the *Confessions* prayed, "Thou hast made us for Thyself, O Lord", he put his finger on the essence of the matter. He established the right order of things by starting with their proper end. What is not God does not exist as if it is to be alien to God, but as if it is to return to Him at the level at which He Himself exists. This is why those texts that tell us that we desire to see God "face to face" do nothing other than reflect the fullness of the trinitarian life, but now as it is seen outside of itself.

The inner life of God is complete in itself. What is not God exists in order to reveal or reflect this inner order insofar as it can be imitated outside of itself. Since what is not God exists because of love and not because of a necessity within the Godhead, the ultimate order of what is not God will be revealed in and for those beings most like unto God. Their purpose will be achieved only after the manner of a freedom that can reject what it is offered. The logic of the inner life of the Godhead, in other words, necessarily entails the risk—yes, the divine risk—of the individual rejection of the divine purpose in the creation of what is not God, including the rejection of one's own being as created for a happiness it does not give itself.

We can look upon this negatively and think that it is a terrible thing to be given a chance to reject God. This view is common and often the basis of accusing God of being the cause of our own sins. But the positive side of this reflection means simply that it is possible for God to create the kind of beings we are—intelligent, free, finite persons—only if we possess the liberty to reject our own end, the highest good to which we can be ordered. If we could not reject it, we could not accept it or choose it freely, the only condition in which it is worth having.

The internal life of the Godhead, then, points to the fullness of the divine being, to its not needing anything other than its own being. This life is a life of a diversity of different Persons in the exchange of the being of God in different relationships—of being received, of being sent back, of loving. God does not first create the cosmos and then, as an afterthought, create the rational being. Rather, the eventual drama of the rational being comes first. The cosmos is the setting in which this vast story unfolds. But the essence of the story is the person who, ultimately, is asked to choose the good that is given to him, that he does not himself create. Because of the very nature of the inner life of God, it cannot be given away except to someone capable of appreciating it. This latter possibility also includes the possibility of rejecting it.

The trinitarian life of God is reflected in what is not God on the vastest of scales, the scales both of cosmos and of history. But the paradigm of the order that we encounter in the world is already found in the Trinity of Persons and their inner relation to one another. We are to imitate the divine order in all ways that it can be imitated—in making, in living, in thinking, in loving. But ultimately the point of contact is where Gift meets gift, where what proceeds out of the inner life of the Godhead meets the inner life of the finite persons who have, in the end, nothing higher to do than to accept a gift, the gift of revelation with its description of the inner life of the Godhead, that which we call the Trinity of Persons: Father, Son, and Spirit.

CHAPTER III

THE ORDER OF THE COSMOS

> The Heavens declare the glory of God and the firmament sheweth his handiwork.
>
> —Psalm 19:1

> What I think the DNA material has done is show that intelligence must have been involved in getting these extraordinarily diverse elements together. The enormous complexity by which the results were achieved look to me like the work of intelligence.
>
> —Anthony Flew, December 15, 2004[1]

> What might have been and what has been / Point to one end, which is always present.
>
> —T. S. Eliot, *Four Quartets*[2]

I

In this chapter, I wish to make a serious argument about the relation of the cosmos, God, and the human purpose.

[1] Roy Abraham Varghese, "The Supreme Science", *The Dallas News*, December 9, 2005.

[2] T. S. Eliot, *Four Quartets* (New York: Harcourt, 1943), "Burnt Norton", 14.

But I wish to do so in a certain lightsome mood. At first sight, the arguments for coherence and interrelatedness of existing things in such a fashion that they reveal order will seem to many to be preposterous. Yet there is a certain consistency of order that bears the thread of truth. This is what I mean by the "order of the cosmos" or the "order of the created universe"—the order, in Aquinas' terms, of the things we discover but did not make.

Let me make the point in this amusing cosmic way. Lucy is looking up at the sky while Charlie Brown looks blankly at her. She says, "I'm counting the suns, Charlie Brown." As she still stares upward, he replies, "That's really the same sun you see, Lucy. It just goes behind the clouds." With a certain scientific wrath, she yells, "And I suppose that the same sun stays lit all day long?" She continues, "Boy, Charlie Brown, I think you must be getting more stupid every day!" With a groan, Charlie simply holds his stomach.

But Lucy continues looking up at the sky. "I've counted forty-eight suns so far, Charlie Brown." Again Charlie explains, "That's a coincidence. There are also forty-eight states in the Union." Lucy replies, "Really? Bet there's some connection!" Her logic continues, "Sure, there is! This is more than just a coincidence." Charlie covers his eyes and says, "Oh no!" Lucy claims, "I've discovered a scientific truth!"

Charlie keeps on insisting that there is only one sun. Lucy replies, "You say there is only one sun, eh, Charlie Brown?" Charlie is puzzled. She demands, "Well, then, explain this, where does it go every night?" Charlie replies, "No place, it. . . ." At this utter lack of logic and cosmology, Lucy laughs heartily, "No place? OH, HO, HO HO HA HA HA!" Charlie just looks at her while she walks away ruefully, saying, "Arguing with Charlie Brown is so useless. He just can't ever be serious."[3] We have it all here, the number of suns in the universe, scientific truth, coincidence and chance, knowledge of the senses, doubt and truth.

Socrates had said, to recall, that what impressed him most in his cosmological studies was not that he found in them earth, air, fire, and water, but that he found mind. The British philosopher Anthony Flew, in his old age, has told us much the same thing. Cicero, the great Roman philosopher and orator, in his essay "On Old Age", wrote similarly: "As I believe, the reason why the immortal gods implanted souls in human beings was to provide the earth with guardians who should reflect their contemplation of the divine order in the orderly discipline of their own lives."[4] Here again is the Platonic connection between the order of soul and the order of things, with but a hint that this order needs to be put into effect. It is not simply automatic or determined.

"For Plato," Joseph Ratzinger wrote, to make the same point in another way, "the category of the beautiful had been definitive. The beautiful and the good, ultimately the beautiful and God, coincide. Through the appearance of the beautiful we are wounded in our innermost being, and that wound grips us and takes us beyond ourselves; it stirs longing into flight and moves us toward the truly Beautiful."[5] What is orderly and beautiful leads to what is order and beauty in itself. We are made in such a way that, on first beholding what this beauty is, in any of its forms or

[3] Schulz, Charles M. *The Complete Peanuts: 1953–54* (Seattle: Fantagraphics Books, 2004), 294–95.

[4] Cicero, *Selected Works* (Harmondsworth: Penguin, 1971), 244.

[5] Joseph Ratzinger, *The Spirit of the Liturgy* (San Francisco: Ignatius Press, 2000), 126.

worldly manifestations, we cannot rest without an explanation and, indeed, without a possession of it after its own manner.

Many modern thinkers, no doubt, usually do not find mind in the cosmos. One suspects, sometimes, that they do not want to find it there, as its presence has too many further implications, especially on how we live. They find only chance, determinism, or chaos. Sometimes, not always, they find mind in themselves. Not a few think that even their own minds are determined such that they cannot be sure that what they know is *what is*. Thus, the mind they find in the universe, if they find one, is their own. The universe yields only themselves to themselves, not something beyond themselves.

The discovery of mind or order in the cosmos apart from ourselves would, clearly, indicate something to which we had to pay attention. Mind calls to mind. It reaches what it cannot go beyond in the other mind without its consent. But even chance, if that is all that is admitted, seems to indicate the unanticipated crossing of things that are following their own orderly paths. To have chance, not everything can be chance. And if everything is determined, why is there a suspicion, particularly an intellectual suspicion, that it is not? How, on its own grounds, could chance even be conceived? Is this very suspicion of intelligence itself determined? Is the suspicion that things are not determined itself determined? What could that possibly mean besides a contradiction, to be determined not to be determined?

It is said, in the scientific searching in the cosmos for alien life, particularly through listening to radio waves from outer space, that what the researchers look for are intelligible constants and deliberately organized patterns that would indicate the presence of mind or intelligence within the message. It is assumed that intelligence would seek intelligence in an intelligent way and that other intelligences would recognize it in an intelligible way. Thus far, evidently, for better or worse, no active minds signaling for the attention of the inhabitants of this planet have been found in spite of extensive investigation to find them. But the mere fact that, by such means, we look for signs of intelligible order indicates that, implicitly, we know what we are looking for. That is, we seek for signs of design, signs of stable constants that evidently hold everywhere in the universe—the speed of light, the definition of a circle, the formulae for life molecules.

Whether or not God is or is not lonely in His inner life, we likewise wonder if, in this infinitely vast created cosmos of which we have some knowledge, we ourselves, as a species, are likewise lonely, utterly alone amid inert or unintelligent beings. Are we, after all, the only living, rational beings in existence, mere accidents? Many claim that, given the vast numbers of planets supposedly in the universe, granted the truth and necessity of what is called "evolution", it is theoretically impossible that no other races of intelligent beings be found in other places in the cosmos. On the other hand, if we are indeed alone in the vast universe, said to contain some 125 billion galaxies, with untold numbers of suns, planets, comets, and moons, it might seem to increase, not lessen, our relative importance. Pascal thought that this vastness not only made us seem insignificant, it even frightened us. But as Chesterton once said, we should never confuse spirit with size. The cosmos may in fact exist for the microcosmos, for man, the being in whom all the levels of creation—matter, vegetable, animal, and spirit—existed, as the ancients also thought.

Not a few indications suggest that we, in our own internal makeup, both physical and especially volitional, are more complex than even the galaxies. I believe that Einstein once remarked that politics was more complicated than physics. When we think about the galaxies, moreover, we know them; they do not know us. Nothing is more startling than this realization. Galaxies as galaxies know nothing. Walker Percy's famous question in his well-entitled book *Lost in the Cosmos* still serves to make this point most vividly: "Why is it possible to learn more in ten minutes about the Crab Nebula in Taurus, which is 6,000 light-years away, than you presently know about yourself, even though you've been stuck with yourself all your life?" [6] The obvious answer to this rhetorical question is that, without downplaying the wonders of the universe, human life is more complicated than the cosmos. Yet human life is itself found within the cosmos. It too is found, not made, by human intelligence, even when human intelligence comes to understand some of the components of its making.

C. S. Lewis' Space Trilogy (*Out of the Silent Planet*, *Perelandra*, and *That Hideous Strength*) has explored the theological dimensions of this probability of other rational beings in the universe with their possible relation to God and to us. Lewis conceived the consequences of different choices that were initially made by different races through their original first parents. Our planet was "silent" to other planets because of the choice of Adam and Eve to reject what was offered to them. We live in the consequences of this free rejection with the addition of the divine response to it that we know as the order of redemption (chapter 8).

[6] Walker Percy, *Lost in the Cosmos* (New York: Washington Square Books, 1983), 7.

However, it is also possible that some other "first parents" someplace else in the universe might not have been offered supernatural life as their constitutive orientation to the Godhead, as was the case with the human race. This other race might have been given existence only as rational beings destined to no higher level than that due to them by nature. They would have continued in the natural state of mankind's own intrinsic level of being subject to the vicissitudes of all finite being. They would have had immortal souls, as Socrates surmised. But they would not live in hope of any beatific vision or resurrection of the body, the revealed purpose of this race to which we belong.

Too, it is possible that some race, unlike our first parents, might have rejected the Devil's temptation and chosen the original graced condition offered to Adam and Eve. This alternative would have placed them in a world without the Fall or death but with supernatural grace to achieve the original end offered, the beatific vision itself. The assumption here, of course, is that Adam and Eve had a real choice that involved both themselves and their progeny as a direct consequence of their choice. We should not underestimate the delicacy of this consideration, as it is what links the highest in man, his own reason and freedom, with the freedom of the Godhead to act outside of Himself.

Likewise, it is conceivable that a damned race might exist, those who simply and freely rejected any of God's terms and chose to live with this rejection, to form their souls by it. It is not without amusement that Lewis chose the academic community itself as the society in which this dire choice is most likely to happen. The point of the rejection of God's free gifts is always the temptation of the human mind to replace the divine mind as man's own perceived and concocted good. Scripture in fact pictures the fallen angels, the highest of the pure spirits less than God, pretty much in this light of a society of those who have rejected the goods offered to them by the Godhead.

The complexity and variability of the universe, Lewis held, was thus not without its theological ramifications. Or perhaps vice versa—that is, the structure of the universe followed upon theological choices. In any case, Lewis' point was that God did not simply create a natural universe and subsequently wonder what to do with it. He did not dream up the universe first, then man. Rather, the universe looked like what He intended to do with it, if He chose to do anything outside of Himself. The universe was made as a home for man wherein to work out his ultimate purpose, the destiny and purpose given to him not by himself but by God. The cosmos, thus, was not simply intended as a display of divine power and majesty, though it was that too. The heavens do declare the glory of God, as the Psalmist says.

II

Thus far, the fact is that we have discovered nothing in the way of finite intelligences outside of ourselves and our own planet's history. Certainly no other rational life seems evident in our solar system. We are now far enough in our scientific and space explorations to be sure of this absence. Though there is no easily attainable theoretic reason that it need be so, the human race is, as far as it is empirically known, alone. Some find this disturbing; others find this exhilarating. The fact is that, even if there were other rational beings in the universe, in some other galaxy, we do not know them. Such possible beings, in spite of all the UFO rumors and space movies, have made no contact with us. And even if they were rational beings more or less like ourselves, we have no assurance that they would know more about ultimate things than we do.

Thus, because of the schema of choices spelled out by Lewis, we have no reason to think that, should contact be made with us by other races of intelligent beings in the universe, it would necessarily be, either for us or them, benign—though, on the same logic, it could be. Space fiction provides both kinds of scenarios, one where we corrupt some other race, the other where they further corrupt us. The lives and destinies of the some hundred billion human beings who have already thus far lived and died on this planet have taken place without the presence or evidence of other terrestrial intelligences in the cosmos. This suggests that we already have our own purpose for existing that does not depend directly on our discovering other minds in the cosmos. If we suddenly did discover intelligent life elsewhere, it would not follow that the lives of our kind up to that point were somehow useless or without purpose.

We are loath to think that these numerous ancestors of ours who knew nothing of extraterrestrial life did not have an opportunity to reach the allotted destiny for which they were created in the first place. Nor does it seem likely that the meaning of past and present human life is dependent on some future cosmic event about which we know nothing. This conclusion seems to be what T. S. Eliot meant about past and future being also in what is present. And even if there were other existing intelligences, we are not sure that they would know more about why we or they exist than what we already know from our own experience and our own reason. Our sun is said to burn at ten thousand degrees Fahrenheit and will last about ten billion years, half of which are already gone. Though there is no immediate rush, we have here no lasting city.

We have noted that, if the inner life of the Godhead is complete in itself, then what is not God need not exist. But if what need not exist does in fact exist, as we see that it does, we seek to account for its order or purpose. Why does it stand out of nothingness? Why is it this configuration and not that? From nothingness, nothing comes. The origin of something existing cannot be, in any strict sense, "nothing". This is one thing of which our minds can be quite sure on their own evidence. When the Psalmist declared that the heavens manifested the glory of God, he also indicated by that very term "glory" that the heavens were not wholly accidental, even if they need not exist in the first place.

T. S. Eliot affirms that what is past and what is present, even what might have been, indicate a *present* purpose. This is a metaphysical point of great depth. That is to say, the cosmos, the order of physical things, includes human things that do not fall under man's free will. This natural universe always does what it is intended to do within its own order. But this characteristic of physical things to follow their own natures in their actions does not mean that there cannot be chance or accident within what is otherwise an order. Chance exists because of order, because of the crossing of two things doing what they are supposed to be doing. The issue of divine providence rightly asks whether even things of chance have a higher order. Accidents do not hinder the order of providence but help to achieve it.

A famous philosophic principle affirms that what is first in intention may be last in execution. Likewise, what is first presented to our attention may, while remaining itself, be of importance primarily insofar as it is the ground, as it were, for something of greater moment. From this point of view, it is possible to think that the vastness of the universe, its apparent complexity, and its amazing age are not the most important things within the confines of time and space. The link between the inner life of the Godhead and the order of the cosmos is to be found at the confluence of what exists outside and inside the Godhead.

The most important thing in the Godhead with respect to a creation that need not exist is this: God fashions and orders what creation itself is about, in all its vastness and complexity. The most significant, and perhaps the most complex, thing in creation is, in fact, the human person and the free achievement of its final end according to the order it is given not by itself. And the physical-spiritual structure of the human corpus may itself be less complicated than man's many purposeful activities taking place through its instrumentality. Is there any way to make sense of such a proposition? Is there any conceivable relationship between a cosmos that is not God and human intelligence that likewise is not God? Is the cosmos for man? And if so, what is man for?

Obviously, much of the scientific world has held for a couple of centuries that no God or intelligent principle or intrinsic design lies behind what exists. Hume had claimed that "the contrary of every matter of fact is possible." This subtle principle by itself, if held to be true, destroyed any notion of a stable order of things, since the opposite of anything we presently know might also be confronting us at the same time. If what is seemingly known for certain can, at the same time, also be its opposite, we can literally know nothing. If intelligence exists in the universe, by implication in this hypothesis, it is a mere accident. It has no cause in itself. Neither the cosmos nor human life is said to reveal any overarching order that could indicate that it arises from a source outside of itself. The human person is not explained as having its ultimate origin in a transcendent, intelligent, trinitarian Godhead. Rather, it came about—so it is postulated—by accident and reveals no purposeful order.

The alternative to a creative order is said to be "evolution", an order presupposed to no order or possible cause. Though it can simply and legitimately mean a way to classify the differing beings that in fact are found to exist over time both in the cosmos and on earth, "evolution" can also mean, and generally does mean, a philosophy of how something comes from nothing. E. F. Schumacher called "evolutionism" the ideology claiming that something comes from nothing over time, especially over a considerable amount of time. But a thing cannot come from nothing no matter how much time it has. If a thing could, with equal logic, come from nothing, it could do so in a second as well as in a trillion years. Schumacher wrote:

> Evolutionism as currently presented has no basis in science. It can be described as a peculiarly degraded religion, many of whose high priests do not even believe in what they proclaim. Despite widespread disbelief, the doctrinaire propaganda which insists that the scientific knowledge of evolution *leaves no room* for any higher faith continues unabated. Counter-arguments are simply ignored. The article on "Evolution" in *The New Encyclopaedia Britannica* (1975) concludes with a section entitled "The Acceptance of Evolution", which claims that "objections

> to evolution have come from theological and, for a time, from political standpoints." Who would suspect, reading this, that the most serious objections have been raised by numerous biologists and other scientists of unimpeachable credentials?[7]

The fact is that today religion is more apt to agree with evolutionism as an ideology than to challenge it. What is of interest is not whether evolutionism is popularly and scientifically held and taught to be true, but whether there is evidence that this theory cannot be sustained insofar as it is claimed that something comes from nothing, that there is no mind found in the universe.

Ironically, in spite of the vast age of the universe, the prime reason science might think that the order of the world is not just by chance is because there simply has not been enough time, on the basis of probability statistics within evolutionary theory itself, for what did happen to come about. The evidence seems to show, rather, that this universe displays remarkable coincidences about the production of planets and stars, enough to indicate that, had things not happened in a very specific and ordered way within very narrow confines of time and space, human life could not have come forth in an environment that could sustain it. In what is known as the "anthropomorphic principle", it looks like the universe itself was designed so that the human being with his own intelligence could appear someplace within it. That the planet earth, with an age of perhaps 4.5 billion years, is the place where it happened does not make the premises of this reflection less significant.

[7] E. F. Schumacher, *A Guide for the Perplexed* (New York: Harper Colophon, 1977), 114.

III

Let us suppose, for the sake of argument, that in fact the universe is not created for itself simply to manifest the vast spaces and rigidly determined beings or particles that inhabit it from the smallest to the largest. This consideration goes back to Aquinas' observation that the internal order of a thing is consequent on its real purpose or external order. It seems odd that the universe would just be floating there with no relation to an intelligible order within it that would indicate why it is as it is. This position implies that the cosmos is not fully explained only in terms of God and the nonhuman aspects of the cosmos. To put it more bluntly, the universe would seem incomplete and incoherent if what existed were only God and physical things within which universe no intelligent being existed to reflect on it or to use it, even to perfect it.

Moreover, it turns out that we find as much complexity in the smallest existing things as we do in the greatest ones. Traditionally, "microcosmos" has been a term used to define man himself. Man is the "small" ordered world. Man is the being in whom all levels of reality—inert matter, vegetable, animal, and spirit—are found combined in an orderly fashion within one whole person or being. Each of the levels of being has its own character or scope. What distinguishes living things from inert matter, with its own diversity, is generally held to be some inner principle of soul or movement whereby the living thing finds and carries out its own inner purpose with the aid of what it finds in the matter surrounding it. It is not just pushed around from outside of itself as in the case of inert matter. A rose grows up to be a rose, not an oak or a toad. If a rosebush suddenly produced a rock one day, then a toad the next, then a tree the next, and this in no order, we would have chaos—that is, no order and no intelligibility.

Animals have more complicated inner principles. Not merely do they live, but they have sensory powers whereby they can move from place to place. The variety of plant and animal life is itself amazing. It reveals an astonishing abundance in things. And through reproduction, the particular species keeps itself in existence. However difficult it may be in extreme cases sometimes to tell the difference between plant and animal life, there is, nonetheless, a radical difference between the two as likewise there is between inert matter and vegetative life. Clearly, plants are not possible without the inert but fertile earth. Animals are not possible without plants or other animals as food.

Each species of animal or plant seems to possess its own natural order in manifesting what it is. No doubt, some plants and animals come to be or cease to be at different stages of the earth's history. Evidently, many species of animals and plants ceased to exist long before there ever were human beings on this planet. We might think this extinction to be a tragedy, but it seems to be nothing more than the earth and the life it carries being what they are. Dinosaurs did not anticipate or plan their becoming extinct.

Human beings subsume or integrate into themselves all of these powers of the beings that are below them. They add one power that is not present in plants or animals. All four levels of being are found within the human, the microcosmos. What is different is that the human person seems to be an ordered whole of all levels—the grades of being seem to exist in an inner harmony. If the person has vegetative powers such as hair and nails, or sensory powers such as sight and hearing, or the faculty of memory, these capacities seem to be ordained to enable him to know. Man is able to abstract from the particular thing he knows to arrive at a general idea of certain kinds of things—roses or toads, for instance. This characteristic power is why Aristotle defined him as precisely the "rational animal". His reasoning and willing powers make it possible for the human being to do many more things than do other beings who live by instinct and whose lives are basically a repetition of a set life cycle.

The human being's capacity to know relates him to all the other creatures that he finds about him. It also causes him to wonder about the meaning of the existences of these things. Without denying the objective goodness or order of nature, nature seems itself to be ordered to the human purpose as if the cosmos or the earth itself flourishes best under care of the rational creature who is free to use nature for his own purpose. In this sense, nature seems ordered to the human purpose and is incomplete without it. Looked at from this angle, the cosmos does not exist for itself, nor directly for its Creator, but rather, it exists as part of an order whose completion is found in the mind of the rational creature and his own purposeful end. Logically, this view means not that man ends in the cosmos, but that the cosmos ends in man.

But when we arrive at this point, we still must inquire whether the human purpose is merely to take care of the earth and of other human beings, though it seems to be at least that. The newest modern "religion" is probably that form of ecology or environmentalism that postulates the purpose of the human race is to keep itself in existence as long as possible, since that is the only ultimate existence open to it. This consideration that cosmic purpose leads to human purpose eventually leads us to pay attention to the order of polity and the order of mind, the activities that are peculiarly human and would not exist in the universe without the existence of finite mind in its human form in some kind of adequate physical setting.

In recent years, the presence of man in the universe, particularly on this planet, has come to be considered by many as something of a threat or a danger to the earth itself. Human purposes are said to be subordinate to earthly purposes. Nothing in what we know of human activity, of course, leads us to suspect that we cannot abuse the earthly condition in which we find ourselves. But the purpose of man in the cosmos is not simply to change nothing that the earth provides so that it remains down the ages in its pristine condition that it supposedly bore before the appearance of man on this planet. The earth's resources and structure seem in fact to have been provided precisely that man could use them for his purposes.

As we have seen in touching on the age of the sun, eventually this earth will collapse into oblivion. That it will probably take a few billion more years does not obviate the principle involved, namely, that no matter what we do, we, as a species, cannot remain on this planet forever. Individually, of course, we pass out of it every day. Several famous space novels or even space projects propose that we find a way to other possibly habitable planets in order to save the tragedy of the complete loss of human life in the universe. There is nothing wrong with such thinking at one level, provided that it becomes feasible. But the more important issue is the relation of the earth to man's purpose. And in this, again, there seems to be at the center of things the presence of mind—this time, human mind.

IV

Here I do not want to consider any supernatural destiny of man, though that too, as we have seen, is central to this discussion. Rather, the primary issue is whether the earth is adequate to provide for human inner-worldly purposes, whether we assume a natural or supernatural destiny. I do not doubt that inner-worldly purposes are themselves in fact ordered to transcendent purposes. The cosmos itself can be included in this transcendent purpose, as Saint Paul seems to suggest. But the issue is whether the resources of the earth are so limited and sparse that we need to grant political control over both our population and consumption to restrict our numbers and activities. For many, this view is a very attractive alternative, as it seems to give a moral purpose to human activity, namely, long-range self-preservation of the race on this planet.

An opposing view would suggest that the purpose of human civilization is not simply to keep the earth and itself in existence. That the earth will cease at some time is simply a fact. Whether we will cease before the earth does is unknown, but probable. The question is whether culture is opposed to environment. I would approach this question again on the basis of the order of cosmos. That is, the existence of the rational animal is not merely an accident in the universe, but it is something that is intended to complete the universe within itself, as it were. The first and essential purpose of this being's existence is his own destiny, which is not, as such, inner-worldly. That is, humanity is not primarily created to keep the world in existence in some pristine condition so that it continues down the ages as long as possible. But I do not want to deny that there is an inner-worldly purpose that provides the background and occasion for the main drama to be played out. Indeed, this drama is itself made possible by the relation of men to men within the context of their earthly existence.

Let me approach this question through the idea of wealth. It is easy to observe that human life requires a certain amount of wealth or property within which its material conditions are provided. But what is wealth? Aristotle had already proposed that wealth is one of the possible definitions of happiness. With wealth, it seemed, we could buy pleasure or honor or other components of this elusive end. However, as Aristotle was shrewd to answer, wealth was not itself happiness. It was at most a means to something else that we really wanted. Yet it was obvious that, because we were physical beings, we required material goods to keep us alive and flourishing. This very natural requirement was itself the basis of the moral justification for man to use what was provided in nature. This relationship again implied a certain order. What was higher in the scale of being was that to which what was lower was ordered.

From this point of view, the history of human life and culture on this planet is the gradual learning of better ways for man to provide what he needs for himself. Following certain themes in Genesis, the earth was created for man and his purposes. He was given dominion over it. This view implied a certain harmony in which the levels of being were related to one another. It was not wrong for animals to eat plants, nor for animals to eat animals, nor for human beings to eat both. Moreover, it was discovered early on, as Locke pointed out, that the earth unattended to was not a very good provider. That is, people who simply lived off of uncultivated earth required much land and patience to be able to collect enough barely to survive. The earth, it was learned, was more fruitful if it could be cultivated in a rational manner. Farms and gardens were more productive than unattended lands. We now even cultivate trees and forests. This experience implied that somehow it was meant to be that the earth be made more fruitful by the addition of human work.

The next question was what sort of land was more productive: that which was cultivated by individual owners or that which was cultivated collectively? Again, both ways were tried and are still tried. The fact was that, generally speaking, individual or private-group cultivation and distribution of what was grown was a more fruitful way to use the earth for human purposes. From the beginning, man had not only his own power available to him, but also that of certain animals, whereby he could be more productive than by himself. Again, this seemed to be natural and purposive. Gradually, particularly in farming and in commerce, wind and water were employed as sources of energy over and above human or animal power.

We know in retrospect that gradually power from steam, coal, gas, and oil came to be used in machinery that replaced animal and human power. Again the question was, what is the source of energy? Coal and oil, however abundant, were themselves products of long eons of vegetative growth on the planet. Besides the energy so stored in the earth, there is direct solar energy that arrives on this planet every day, together with nuclear and hydrogen sources. In referring to these and other sources, what is to be noted is that the term "scarcity" of energy is itself a transitory notion. Energy is scarce or inefficient only if we limit ourselves to one or another kind of energy, say, coal or oil, and not hydrogen or solar power. Energy is available to us to the degree that we know what is available and know how to use it.

The real energy or source of wealth is not, in the end, something finite like coal or oil supplies, but rather, the knowledge of how to use such sources. The day will undoubtedly come when oil is so expensive that we cannot afford it, but no doubt on that day other energy sources will have been developed so that oil becomes relatively useless. The ultimate energy, in other words, is the human mind and its capacity to apply what it knows. In this sense, the human race is not confronted with a resources problem, but with a mind problem. There is no shortage of energy. There may be a shortage of "mind" in the sense of unwillingness to use what we know or invent what we do not. But objectively speaking, we have unlimited sources of energy. The human race is not limited because there is not enough energy available to it. It may be limited by its willingness to think of how to use energy well or how to produce it. But that is another kind of problem.

If this be the case, then the question of the purpose of the cosmos again comes into view. That is, the purpose of man in the universe is not simply to preserve the earth in its pristine state. Rather, it is to see what man can do to improve and beautify the earth with all the available powers that he has been given to develop. One might even say that the purpose of the earth is, in fact, to be beautified, a subject to which we will turn later (chapter 9). This again is the Platonic theme that we are to imitate the gods, to reflect their order in our order, to be moved by what is lovely.

V

We can look upon the cosmos from the point of view of its age in billions of years or of its extent in billions of light-years. These are worthy considerations. But since it is we who are measuring and asking about time and space, it is clear that time and space themselves ask nothing of themselves or of us. Moreover, when we examine these conditions of time and space, we find the curious calculations that indicate that the planet on which human life exists could have come into existence only if many intricately convergent events and principles in the broader and vaster universe came together. The harmony suggested by Psalm 8 seems, when spelled out, not only poetic, but almost scientific. "When I consider thy heavens, the work of thy fingers, the moon and the stars, which thou hast ordained; what is man, that thou art mindful of him? . . . For thou has made him a little lower than the angels, and hast crowned him with glory and honour. Thou madest him to have dominion over the works of thy hands; thou put all things under his feet." The relation of Creator, cosmos, and man, in terms of mutual purpose, is not without evidence.

"For the secret of man's being is not only to live but to have something to live for", we read in Dostoevsky's famous passage from "The Grand Inquisitor".

> Without a firm conception of the object of life, man would not consent to go on living, and would rather destroy himself than remain on earth, though he had bread in abundance. That is true. But what happened? Instead of taking men's freedom from them, you [Christ] made it greater than ever! Did you forget that man prefers peace, and even death, to freedom of choice in the knowledge of good and evil?[8]

[8] Fyodor Dostoevsky, *Notes from Underground; The Grand Inquisitor* (New York: Dutton, 1960), 129.

Probably no passage more graphically states what is at stake in the proper understanding of the cosmos, its order, and its relation to the human enterprise on earth. The passage displays the connection of the transcendent to this world as the scene of the drama of man's own destiny.

Men, Dostoevsky suggests, would rather destroy themselves, even if they had a sufficiency of food and presumably other things, than to live merely to stay alive as if that staying alive were the only good to which all else is to be sacrificed. We need not only to live, but to have something for which to live. Does the order of the cosmos suggest that the cosmos itself is what is worth living for? Is the mapping and exploration of space sufficient to explain us to ourselves? Does the continuation of life on the planet suggest that even this purpose is what is worth living for?

The only thing that is worth living for falls in the realm of what the Inquisitor conceives to be what no man wants. Men are afraid of a choice that accepts that they are really free. What the universe is about is this: to provide a place within its vast confines wherein free and rational lives capable of choosing between good and evil, are both possible and actually exist. These choices alone are ultimately significant because, as we will see, they make a final difference before the Good itself (chapter 7).

When we cross the line of being from the plant and animal kingdom, we begin to see that the human species, the billions of individuals who have lived on this green earth over time, has lived as individual persons, each with his own story and personal destiny. The human being is the one being in the physical cosmos that seems to exist for himself because he can see the whole and its relation to him. In a Wendell Berry short story entitled "Light and Warmth", we read:

> "That old boy of Grover's didn't have brains enough to hold his ears apart, did he?"
>
> "Aw, they've educated him since he got to flying."
>
> "They may have trained him. They haven't educated him."
>
> They laugh, and then Big Ellis, his voice so gentle and generous as to allow even Billy Gibbs a place on earth and in Port William, says: "Well, a fellow ought to think the best he can of a fellow oughtn't he? Old Billy, he was a little chuckleheaded and wild, but that's just a boy, ain't it?"[9]

To be allowed "a place on earth" wherein to work out the distinction of good and evil is what, in the end, the cosmos and earth seem to be about. No doubt, once this destiny is chosen, it continues in what it is. One choice is to be enclosed within oneself for eternity; the other is to be open to all things not oneself. If the cosmos is ultimately in existence as the physical arena of the relation between the rational being and his ultimate origin, it remains the arena after the choice, however we are to understand this, even though the first choice is the reception of the gift of the inner life of the Godhead, the reason for the existence of what is not God in the first place. Aquinas, in his discussion of Aristotle's notion that the cosmos was eternal, argued that although the cosmos had a beginning in time, there was nothing contradictory in the notion of God choosing to create a finite universe from eternity. Its essence would remain finite under God's power.

Whatever be the arguments for the resurrection of the body, they converge on the fact that man is not whole without a body and hence without a cosmos in which it is to

[9] Wendell Berry, "Light and Warmth", in *A Place on Earth: A Revision* (New York: Farrar, Straus, and Giroux, 1983), 80.

continue. Thus Paul says in his Letter to the Romans: "Creation itself will be set free from its bondage to decay and obtain the glorious liberty of the children of God. We know that the whole creation has been groaning in travail together until now; and not only the creation, but we ourselves, who have the first fruits of the Spirit, groan inwardly as we wait for adoption as sons, the redemption of our bodies" (8:21–23). Again, we find here the curious relation of God, freedom, cosmos, and the human person's destiny. Such things do belong together in some coherent whole.

CHAPTER IV

THE ORDER OF SOUL

And in some of the people in the town and the community surrounding it, one of the characteristic diseases of the twentieth century was making its way: the suspicion that they would be greatly improved if they were someplace else.

—Wendell Berry, *That Distant Land*[1]

Thus, in moral discussions it is to be remembered that many impediments obstruct our practice, which very easily give way to theory. The speculatist is only in danger of erroneous reasoning, but the man involved in life has his own passions, and those of others, to encounter and is embarrassed with a thousand inconveniences, which confound him with a variety of impulse, and either perplex or obstruct his way.

—Samuel Johnson, May 5, 1750[2]

It's ridiculous, isn't it, to strain every nerve to attain the utmost exactness and clarity about other things of little value and not to consider the most important things worthy of the greatest exactness?

—Plato *Republic* 504d

[1] Wendell Berry, "Pray Without Ceasing", in *That Distant Land: The Collected Stories* (Washington: Shoemaker and Hoard, 2004), 49.

[2] Samuel Johnson, *The Rambler: Selected Essays* (Harmondsworth: Penguin, 2003), 40.

I

The view expressed in Wendell Berry's novel that we would be "greatly improved" if we were "someplace else", a position that Berry thinks undermines the very notions of self, family, and community, must be read in the light of the Platonic teaching that the order of our polity reflects the prior order (or disorder) of our souls. If we wish to improve the world, the place to begin is not "someplace else", with institutions or cultures, but with ourselves, within where we actually live innermost to ourselves. And "improvement" means that we can distinguish between mere change and the attainment of what is actually better. But even if we might know what is humanly better, it by no means follows that we will either choose to or be able to achieve it once we know and choose it. More is at stake than will or decision, but nothing happens without either.

As Samuel Johnson said, based on wide experience of human nature, "a thousand inconveniences" and a "variety of impulses" can and often do impede our achieving what we understand to be worthy accomplishments even when we resolutely choose to strive for them. Still, while not denying the significance of small things, some things are more important than others. The essence of civilization is to know the difference. We instinctively suspect, as Plato intimated, that something is wrong with our paying too little attention to the most important things. Yet, in some delicate way, little things usually remain intertwined with the important things.

Chesterton, in his introductory essay to *All Things Considered*, "The Case for the Ephemeral", wrote: "Brief as is the career of such a book as this, it may last just twenty minutes longer than most of the philosophies that it attacks.

In the end it will not matter to us whether we wrote well or ill; whether we fought with flails or reeds. It will matter to us greatly on what side we fought."[3] Great events often have insignificant beginnings, as Aristotle said. Great issues are always decided first in obscurity, wherein we decide for whom we will fight, for what we will stand. Manners and morals belong together. The external order of polity, economy, culture, or religion does make a difference in how we act and think, without determining us or lessening the power of our own self-rule.

Someone once told me of a homily he heard at a university chapel in which the thesis was proposed that God loves us no matter what we do. We are right to take such advice, however pious its source, most cautiously. We can understand this admonition in two ways. If God loves us literally "no matter what we do", then we might easily conclude that we can do whatever we want. Since, on this hypothesis, nothing we could do would cause God *not* to love us, we do not have to worry about our actions or their consequences. "*Pecca fortiter*", as Luther, perhaps with some exaggeration, was said to have exclaimed—"Sin courageously." This advice, however, is as apt a formula for the libertine as for the ascetic with no obvious grounds for distinguishing the one from the other. Our subjective intentions do not obliterate the objective standards that govern things.

The second way of looking at this admonition is to hold that neither God's love nor His providence ceases just because we freely sin, which we are at liberty to do, given the kind of good but fallen beings we are. God does not change

[3] G.K. Chesterton, *All Things Considered* (New York: Sheed and Ward, 1958), 8.

even if we do. But His love, because the freely chosen disorder in our souls implies a rejection of what is humanly proper, is now a fierce, burning, cleansing force designed precisely to restore our ways to those of order. Within intellectual history we can always find a soft theory of love. On the basis of sincerity, compassion, or tenderness, it dispenses with objective measures by which we distinguish what is worthy and what is unworthy, what is worth fighting for and what is not. Sincerity, compassion, and tenderness have justified many crimes in seeking to excuse or "understand" the wrongdoer. Though this dubious justification is the effect of concentrating on subjective feelings or sentiments, these feelings cannot, it seems, be used to make of what is evil to be good or to make of what is good to be evil. The heinousness of something is not a condition of the sincerity with which we do it.

When we look at the order that we find in the Godhead or in the cosmos, we are seeking, however we come to know them, for signs that are simply there, not of our own making. What it is to be a complete (or incomplete, for that matter) human being is not simply something invented by human beings themselves. What-it-is-to-be-a-human-being is not itself a human formulation, though it can be known or discovered by the human mind.

When we speak of order in our own souls, however, we have a twofold task before us. The first is likewise to determine whether nonarbitrary standards of free human behavior exist, standards that include the possibility of their being freely rejected. That is, are there norms the opposite of which would be also equally acceptable, equally human, equally valid? Is there a difference between a tyrant and a saint? If there is no difference, of course, no standards can exist or be upheld. Is whatever we do justified on the sole grounds that we do it, whatever it is? To be a complete human being, however, following Socrates, and reiterated by Christ, we must affirm that it is never right to do wrong. What it is to do "wrong" or what it is to do "right" is not something arbitrary. Both have a known and unchanging structure. God Himself is not pure, arbitrary will, as not a few philosophies and religions have maintained.

The second enterprise is to decide whether we live up to these standards, once they are understood and established. It is never right to *do* wrong and it is never right intellectually to make what is wrong to be our legitimate standard of living and to justify that course of action. Thus, once we realize that these standards may not be observed by a given human being—that is, he may observe them or not observe them—a twofold order must follow. The first might be called the "order of disorder", the other the "order of order" or the "order of virtue". Under this heading, both orders are looked upon as existing not by necessity, but by choice. One or the other will inevitably flow from our decisions.

In both of these latter cases, when we observe or when we reject the standard in our thought and action, we deal with something that occurs in the world only because the human being, in his free activities, exists in the world. Here we find the realm of human freedom seen in acts put into existence by our choices. These choices need not exist; we could have done something else in each instance of their coming to be. Each of them, until the instant of their doing, could have been otherwise. This fact that they could have been otherwise, but that we make them to be this way or that, is the foundation for our responsibility for them, why we can be praised or blamed for them.

This area of reality, of human acts that are but need not be, as distinct from others, is what is generally understood to be the sphere of morality or ethics. This arena includes acts, invisible in themselves but no less real, that are placed in the world through human choices and the carrying out of those choices. This order, put into existence by human beings acting in their own freedom, is the locus of the specifically human things, things that need not exist, but do. The best order of soul is something that should exist but need not. In fact, most of human experience testifies to its rarity. All real drama and risk in the world are based on this possibility of something initially not needing to exist, but when it does, the consequences follow from the act.

No drama exists in an absolutely deterministic world, only the carrying out of what must be. What we consider as needing to exist are the consequences flowing from free acts, both good and evil, once they are chosen and put into effect. Broadly speaking, ethics deals with putting these actions into reality; history deals with understanding what they were and what followed from them once they were put into being. We do not understand free human acts, either those we are about to perform or those that have been completed, unless we understand them as freely aligning themselves for or against the norm of what is good order. This is why all human actions are worthy of praise or blame because of the content freely put into them by the human decision that brought them about in the first place.

II

How do we approach this question of the "order of soul" when we are considering a right order that ought exist but perhaps does not? Basically, what this twofold possibility implies is a description of human action in such a fashion that we can praise or blame any action on objective grounds. It is not possible to do a free action that is not worthy of praise or blame in actual circumstances. Such praise or blame, of course, implies that someone outside (or ourselves as observers of ourselves) looks at the action and intellectually sees its intrinsic form, meaning, or order. Praise and blame do not cause the action to be good or evil, but acknowledge the action's intrinsic nature.

Much contemporary moral theory wants to eliminate this objective aspect of ethics on the ground that we cannot impose our values on others. This position is but another way of claiming no standard exists that is applicable to all men. But the question is not one of imposing but of recognizing what is already there. We should also recognize that no human action, even the worst, will not be chosen in the name of some presumed good. Every human action will actually contain some good, however convoluted. Evil is always a lack of a good that should be there amid a larger good of the whole. The missing good is not present because we did not put it there where it ought to be. We put into the world acts that lack what ought to be there for them to be whole.

We find in the classical authors, notably Plato, Aristotle, and Cicero, a generally accurate description of the right order of soul that pertains to human life insofar as the human mind by its own powers can understand it. Following the Thomistic principle that "grace builds on nature", we can outline this "natural" human functioning with regard to acts over which we are expected to have control or rule. This natural order of soul is itself set within the higher purpose as proposed by revelation for which men were originally brought into being, namely, their destiny to participate in the inner life of the Godhead. This participation does not by nature belong to human beings, but it is something to which they are now ordered, again as a gift.

This end, higher than that due to human nature, does not destroy the natural virtues but reaffirms and elevates them so that they too, by being what they are, contribute to this higher end. To put it paradoxically, one can lose his soul by seriously failing to perform a natural virtue—courage, say, or temperance, or justice. Natural virtues are not insignificant because they are not supernatural. But they do become elements in our reaching an end higher than we might anticipate by our natural powers. They are not only worth having, but they are necessary to have as elements of the soul in its wholeness.

In practice, we have one life and one "ordered" order, but we can and should distinguish the sources of what we know. Does the knowledge we consider come from reason or revelation or is it found in both? Lack of clarity is not a virtue. We do not read in Aristotle, for instance, the admonition, "Take up your cross daily and follow Me." Aristotle is reason, the latter is revelation, though not contradictory to reason. We do find Aristotle, however, telling us to be just and temperate, even to be brave enough to lay down our lives for what is noble. Even though he did not know revelation, we need not understand Aristotle's philosophy to be in principle "closed" to what is found in revelation. Nor does the notion of revelation forbid us to do what we are advised to do in experience and reasonable judgments. The Ten Commandments have a striking resemblance to what we read in Plato or Aristotle about how we should live. This resemblance is not surprising because what is learned by our rational reflection on ourselves discovers what we are, what it is to be a human being. We are the beings called to fulfill all their capacities, natural and supernatural.

The first thing we need to do, then, is to indicate what "self-rule" means in human life. Once we have some general idea of what self-rule implies, we will begin to see what order of soul means. The first distinction to be made is between those things in the human being over which he has no causal responsibility and those over which he does. Human beings, for instance, generally have two legs, a capacity to be angry, the power to speak, and a sense of fairness. While it is good that we have these capacities, we cannot be said to cause them to exist in ourselves. While we are grateful for having them, we are not their origins. They are given by whatever it is that causes us to be human beings and not toads. The order of soul of which we speak in this chapter does not refer to such things over which we have no control, such as the color of our eyes or the fact that we can speak. It does deal with what we do say when we do speak. What we look to here are those things over which we have some, though not necessarily complete, control such that we are praised or blamed for how we conduct ourselves in this or that matter.

We can give a fairly complete list of things within us by nature over which, nonetheless, we have or ought to have some control or rule. Thus, I define ethics or morality as "the rule of ourselves, in those things in ourselves over which we ought to have some control, more or less, at the right time, in the right place, and in the right circumstances." To rule ourselves, in other words, means to use our mind and will to know and guide what is already in us or related to us so that we direct these powers to a proper purpose, to the end of our being. The question of what is the proper purpose is usually the first thing that we need to attend to. This is the question of what is our end as a mortal human being, in this life, living four score years and ten, or whatever is given to us. We are to present ourselves as complete, ordered, and reasonable beings who show mastery over their actions and passions.

Generally, the end of human life, that is, the reason given for doing everything and anything that we do, is called happiness. Happiness is implicit in each particular choice about what we do. Each particular free action of whatever type or virtue is seen as a means to this defining purpose. In the beginning, we should not expect too much certainty about what exactly we mean by this happiness, though we can gain some knowledge by observing what human beings usually do to explain their actions. Just because all men act to be happy does not mean that all men have an accurate idea of what happiness is. That idea too must be examined and refined. Over time and across cultures, we surprisingly find a consistent response or series of responses. What is confusing is that these responses usually number four or so possible ways to define this happiness and thus guide our actions to accomplishing it. Aristotle has well spelled out these possibilities. The four possible motivations are these: pleasure, honor, wealth, and contemplation. For the most part, all definitions of happiness, in all cultures and in all eras, can be reduced to a variant of one or another of these ends.

A good reason can be found, moreover, why each of these choices might be a candidate. Aristotle discusses each of them and gives the reason why each might be considered. Nothing is chosen without some valid reason. In the end, he selects contemplation as the real definition of happiness, as it is always chosen for its own sake. Contemplation deals with that power which makes men different from other corporeal beings. Pleasure is something that accompanies every human action but varies according to the activity in which it exists. Honor is something that is worthy, the acknowledgment of merit, but we cannot give it to ourselves. Wealth too is good but in and of itself will not make us happy. We always have to use it for what we think will make us happy.

The use of the highest faculty, the mind, to know and to delight in the truth is what Aristotle thinks that both the human corpus and human society are ordained to make possible and foster. All other varieties of definition are some combination or variant of these four. The point is empirical. That is, we know people, including ourselves, who do all they do for one or other of these reasons. This phenomenon appears recurrent everywhere in time and space. The reason why the same moral and intellectual issues recur in all cultures and histories is because through individual births and deaths there is found a constant reappearance of existing individual human persons who form the basis of all moral, societal, and intellectual considerations. What it is to be human abides over time and explains our contact both with our ancestors and with those who follow us.

The next question is, If we do everything for happiness, what is it we do? Briefly, Aristotle says that we perform "the activities of the virtues". Virtues are means to enable us to acquire the sort of happiness we choose as our end. Obviously, there are a number of virtues corresponding to each of those things found in us that need to be and can be ruled in one way or another. "To rule" here means to use our minds and wills to control within reasonable limits what we find can cause us to be praised or blamed. On self-inspection, we find in each of us a number of capacities that we have that need our direct attention to master.

What are these capacities or objects that need attention in order that we might be called "good" through ruling ourselves? These are our fears or pains, our pleasures, our honors, our relation to others, our anger, our property or wealth, our wit, our speech, and our manners. Each of these objects is given to us with our nature or related to it, as in the case of property. These capacities or things given to us by nature we simply find already present in us. Nonetheless, each needs and is open to direction, or rule, as I prefer to call it.

"To rule", that is, to implant rational order, is what we need to do in ourselves, in our families, in our polities—indeed, in any institution. Not to rule ourselves or to rule ourselves badly results in our inability to be what we are intended to be. When we fail to meet the desired or intended order, we are blamed. The same power, our intellect looked upon as guiding our capacities—our practical intellect, as it is called—rules over different immediate objects of self, family, and city. To rule is to put a form of action in some aspect of our activities so that we guide the action according to the norm we select to rule ourselves in this or that area.

Thus, we can say that the practical intellect is designed to rule our passions and our relations to others. The "practical intellect" means our one intellect looked on as governing our actions or makings. It is what indicates what the order is that we will or choose to follow in our actions. All three objects go together as we are talking about human beings ruling themselves, their families, and their polities. In some sense, all three areas of life need to be properly ordered for us to be what we are intended to be and, hopefully, want to be.

"Authority" simply means or refers to what decides what it is that we will do in this or that particular instance to accomplish our end by this chosen means. In us, authority is reason. In the family, it is the parent. In the polity, it is the legitimate ruling principle. Practical intellect, be it noted, does not mean that we have two intellects; rather, it refers to our one intellect looked at as actively governing its own actions or makings in particular human circumstances. Practical intellect deals with things that can be otherwise, that need not exist in one given way. It is contrasted with "speculative intellect", or "theoretical intellect", which is our same intellect used simply to know things in their truth, to know *what is.* Ethics, politics, art, rhetoric, and family rule are matters primarily of practical intellect, of putting order into souls that can do things otherwise.

A virtue is a good habit, while a vice is a bad habit. A habit is a deliberate modification or guiding of what we do or think so that we do it easily and efficiently. A habit is acquired by repeated actions on the object of the virtue—say, on our fears in the case of courage. Thus, when we acquire a virtue, we are easily able both to recognize that we are confronted with a problem concerning our fears or pains and that we can rule ourselves to do what needs or ought to be done in the particular instant in which we must choose. It is in these choosings that our particular character is manifested. "Character" means that particular combination of virtues and vices or habits that we have, but it also includes all the possible areas over which we should rule ourselves. A virtue is thus a mean between the two extremes of too much and too little. But it is not a kind of mathematical formula. It depends on the virtue of prudence, the intellectual virtue of the moral virtues, to determine just what is the situation before us. Prudence, then, is present in every act of every virtue, guiding the act toward our defined and chosen end of happiness.

An ordered soul, therefore, will carefully examine each object or power within it and seek to rule it, that is, impose its prudential intellect on the act. This act is seen in the light of the soul's end. It is to be noted that if we choose the wrong end, which we can, all our "virtues" will be conceived as guiding our particular acts of whatever area—courage, temperance, justice, anger—to this end, according to which we define our happiness. In this paradoxical sense, virtues can aid the effective accomplishment of vices. In other words, we can learn to rob a bank well—something that actually makes the fault or sin worse.

Once we have understood that we have these capacities and that we need to look to their rule, we can begin and complete the task of self-rule over our souls. It is not necessary to think that we need no outside help here from the instructions of the wise, or from the law of the polity, or from the examples of our families, or even from grace. But we can and should try to figure out what is before us to accomplish. We should begin with that as yet unruled area within our souls that is open to the stamp of our practical intellect guiding us, if we choose, to a proper end.

III

We are asking about the order of our own souls. In one sense, this represents the prime order, which, if gotten wrong, will cause probably all else to be distorted. We can look upon ourselves as directing ourselves to our own happiness. First we must, either implicitly or explicitly, decide what this happiness is. We next have to put into effect means or decisions by which we hope to accomplish this end. It turns out that in order to achieve the highest end for which we are made, all else in us needs to be more or less in order. In general, ethical endeavors describe our chosen activities by which we seek in each circumstance to achieve this end. Suppose that we have made our final definition of happiness to be pleasure, for instance. It is possible to do this. It follows that each of our particular actions will be designed in one way or another to achieve this purpose on the assumption that this is what human happiness consists in for us. Pleasure is itself a good thing but not necessarily the proper or whole definition of happiness. It takes an intellectual examination to consider and place it in its proper place within the soul.

The opposite of the virtues are the vices. "Virtue" and "vice" refer to possible action with regard to the same object; that is, we either are just or unjust about our relations to others, temperate or intemperate about our pleasures. Generally speaking, once we have acquired a virtue or a vice, we do not much consider further how we will act. A habit is, in a way, a willed prechoice whereby we dispose ourselves to acting well or ill. However, ordinarily, most people are not either completely virtuous or vicious but are in-between. That is, if we look at their character, at what they habitually do, we see that often they do the right thing or often the wrong thing. But sometimes they can do the opposite of what we expect of them. This possibility means that they are not yet totally set in their ways.

Most people, most of the time, fall within these categories, normally called "continence" when they usually do the right thing, and "incontinence" when they usually do the wrong thing. This intermediate condition, found in all moral areas, is a significant point when we consider the order of the polity. Most polities are usually composed of those neither perfectly virtuous nor completely vicious. It is also possible to conceive of those of superhuman virtue or superhuman vice, since we witness such things in experience and history. They are exceptions but need to be acknowledged as possible.

In discussing the rule of ourselves over ourselves, we want to identify first where we are and whether we intend to become better or worse by some objective standard of better and worse. We are, in a sense, a project to ourselves. We are making ourselves into what we choose to be. We want to know how we deal with our pleasures, with our fears and pains, with our anger, with our property, with our wit, with the honor due to us, with our telling the truth, with our manners, and with our fair relations to others. These are the objects of the virtues, each of which is part of a whole internal order of soul.

Any of these virtues, moreover, can involve some relation to other people and hence can fall under the consideration of justice, which is both its own virtue and is included in any relation of any virtue to others. Thus, temperance can be something that concerns ourselves alone, but when we fail to be temperate—say in drinking—we can jeopardize others. Then the same virtue, temperance, also becomes a question of justice. That is, it relates us to others because our lack of virtue impinges on them. The vice of intemperance, in such a case, becomes also the vice of injustice.

Justice is the great virtue that relates us to other people in the question of how we stand to them, say, whether we return what we owe. Justice is generally considered to be something that simply relates us to one another, or to the community. In the latter case, it is called "distributive justice". We want to know whether we are proportionately awarded or punished for what we contribute or do not contribute to the community to which we belong. Justice with regard to another individual is concerned with whether, in our relations with him, we "render what is due", which is the classical definition of justice.

Justice is a harsh virtue in a way, since it does not look primarily to the person or his internal qualities but simply to the relationship of what is or is not owed to another. We owe justice even to those we do not know or care about, even to our enemies. Under the aspect of being involved with others either because of an accident or because we choose voluntarily to enter a relationship with them, we are potentially related to any given human being in the world with whom we may come in contact. While justice is often considered to be the political virtue, Aristotle himself recognizes that there is something incomplete about it. This is why he devotes more time and space to friendship than to justice.

Friendship and contemplation are the crowning considerations in any ethical or moral life because they provide the context in which the highest things can exist among human beings, insofar as this is possible. The moral virtues themselves have their own order to each other. The virtue of courage, by which we rule our fears and pains, is designed to keep us in being. It is ordered to the good of our existing as we are. Once we exist and exist in good health, the various pleasures that come to us from food, sex, smell, hearing, and touch—in general, from every one of our senses—needs itself to be identified and guided. The soul is not designed to deny but to acknowledge that pleasure is pleasure, though each pleasure falls within the purpose of the act in which it exists.

A considerable amount of intellectual effort goes into establishing the good and validity of the various pleasures. Basically, every activity has its own proper pleasure designed to enhance or foster the activity's own purpose. Pleasure itself is never wrong. What is wrong is the improper use of it for a purpose that distorts its own good, the good of the activity in which it exists. This possibility of separating pleasure from the good in which its act consists is what makes it possible to identify pleasure with happiness.

The purpose of the human mind, that which makes the "rational animal" rational, is to identify and know the truth. A free human act must be voluntary and not done out of ignorance, passion, or force. We need to deliberate what real alternatives are available to us here and now to do in fact, not just dream of some impossibility that would be nice but could never happen. Basically, the order of the soul wants each act to be placed there in a proper order with a purpose. But it is true that the moral virtues are also designed to enable us to know and practice what are called the "theoretical virtues", or "speculative virtues". The speculative virtues—wisdom, first principle, and science—are intended simply to cause us to know something for no other reason than to know it, to know *what something is.*

The intellectual or speculative virtues concern the proper order and activity of the mind itself in its knowing. They establish what it is to know or to prove something to be true. "Wisdom" is the knowledge of all things in their balance. "First principle" has to do with that which grounds all thinking, namely, the principle of contradiction. If this principle (a thing cannot be and not be at the same time) is not true, nothing is true. We know it is true by trying to deny it. If we try to deny it, we in that very act affirm it. If something can be its very opposite at the same time that it is itself, then we can really know nothing about reality. "Science" means the argument by which we begin from what is known and argue through the syllogism to what is not yet known. These intellectual virtues order our very thinking so that it may achieve the purpose of the intellect, which is to know the truth of things. Truth is when our minds conform to what we find in reality. We are to say of *what is* that it is, and of *what is not*, that it is not.

There are two kinds of practical "truths", the truth of craft or art and the truth of prudence. The first shows us that something a craftsman makes is "true" when it conforms to what he intended to make, say, a chair. The world is such that we can modify it by the work of our hands and minds. If the craftsman intended to make a chair but ends up with a table, he is not a very good craftsman. But if he intended to make a fine chair and in fact makes one because he used his reason and hands to guide his making, then, if the chair is solid and handsome, we call him a good artist or craftsman. Art is the habit by which we put into existence things that need not exist but do exist because they fulfill a human need or purpose. Art deals with something to be made. Poetry is made of words, music of sounds, sculpture of stone, and automobiles of all sorts of definite things. In each case, what is made comes forth from the maker, who need not as such be a good man in making, say, a good chair, but he needs to be skilled at making.

"Prudence" is the use of the mind to rule those things in us that are open to human governance, those things by which we are called good or bad as human beings. Prudence as such refers to the intellect as it is looking at the possibilities before us of being just, temperate, courageous, mild, or generous. Generally, we have many ways we can do something. We are not restricted to just one way. Within each way is a variety of circumstances. What the mind does is first take a look at what is available for it to do in choosing means to an already chosen end. This end is, in fact, the definition of happiness already decided by the person making the decision about means to achieve it. When the situation before him is understood, the person, with the aid of the will, decides to do this or that particular thing. This is where rightness or wrongness comes in, in the thoroughness with which this prudential judgment is made about what it is doing.

We might wonder just how it is that we can err in the first place, since this possibility is what causes much of the drama of existence. "Evil" means to put something into existence, including a human act, that lacks something that ought to be there to be complete. There is a simple, but subtle, process that we go through whereby we decide what is to belong or not to belong to this act that we are performing here and now. For anyone to praise or blame us for the acts that we put into the world, we have to have freely decided to do this rather than that. In the process of so considering, we become aware of what we do. This process is called by the technical term "double syllogism".

What does the double practical syllogism involve? We are aware, for example, that the issue before us is to do either this or that action, for this or that purpose. The double syllogism explains the usually implicit reasoning process that we go through in choosing to do one action rather than another.

Suppose we have two pieces of cake, one for me and one for my brother. The cake is a favorite, and I am quite hungry. Thus, the cake is objectively pleasurable. It is also true that in justice one piece belongs to me and one to my brother. Suppose, while my brother is absent, I come upon the two pieces of cake. I say, "I am very hungry." This may be true. Or I say, "This is my favorite cake, and it is really delicious." This is also true.

Suppose I eat my piece and find it delicious. No problem. The cake is mine and is delicious. Let us suppose that I do not eat the other piece of cake but leave it for my brother because it is his. I have thus been just. My brother can trust me to do the right thing even when he knows that I like the cake that is his. On the other hand, let us suppose that I do eat the cake that belongs to my brother. What is it that I have done, intellectually, that explains my action and decides my moral responsibility in terms of good or bad?

Basically, there are two implicit syllogisms, or arguments. One says something like: "All just things are to be observed. This cake is my brother's in justice. Therefore I will leave it for him." But there is another possible syllogism: "All chocolate cake is delicious. This is chocolate cake; therefore I will eat it." Now, the cake is delicious. That is the truth. But what I have done is use my intellect to focus on the second syllogism, or the argument about pleasure. I ignored the first syllogism about justice, which pertains to the same object, the cake.

If I am asked why I did what I did, I will say I did it because the cake was good, which it was. I have not lied here. I have given a reason. But I have deliberately not allowed the justice question to enter my thinking. So I put a "lack" of justice into the action that should be objectively there. My brother, when he sees what I did, knows that I have failed to take his property into account. My action causes him to doubt my virtue of justice and makes him angry at me because of something I deliberately did.

What I deliberately did was refuse to see the whole objective situation with the cake as both something belonging to someone else and as being good. All moral disorder takes this form. It consists in suppressing a factor, an argument that would place the whole picture before us. Focusing on the act we want to do, we put a "lack" into the world, as it were. This is why we are responsible and why the act is evil—the act lacks something that ought to be there, and it is we who chose not to put it there.

IV

To understand more fully what is meant by the order of soul, we must see not merely what there is within us that needs to be ruled, what it means to rule, how we go about deciding what to do, the reasons that may mitigate or affirm our responsibility, and what pleasure is. We also need to see our highest activity and the context in which it is best accomplished. Man is by nature a political animal—we will see something more of that in the following chapter on the polity. But there is a sense in which, while not denying its worthiness, man transcends the polity while being within it. The polity makes possible the wide variety of human goods that are possible to put into existence because of the diverse energies and talents of many citizens and the potentiality of the world to be open to human activities. On the other hand, the polity is not itself something that thinks or knows pleasure or pain except through the individual persons who make it up. The highest life takes place when the moral virtues are in order or in place, when we are free from our own disorders of soul so that we can be about what are called the "highest things".

The highest things exist in friendship and in contemplation. At its best, the human being exists to converse with his friends, wherein each seeks to know the truth and to know that he knows it by those criteria by which truth is known. The moral virtues—the rule of ourselves over those things in ourselves subject to our rule—bring us to a point wherein we can really be friends and, at the same time, contemplate the truth of things. Again, in looking at what is the proper order of soul, we do not maintain that most people, most of the time, do have fully ordered souls. We have to know what an ordered soul is to know what, technically, a disordered soul is. Much of our human occupation with one another is, in fact, the effort to discuss and inquire about what is worthy and what is not. It is not a vice to know what vice is. Indeed, it is a vice *not* to know what vice is. The perfection of human knowing includes the proper knowing of the disorders of the human soul in its choices.

Friendship is not itself a virtue, but it involves virtue. What does this mean? Friendship, like justice, relates us to others. There are degrees of friendship, as it were. We can be friends of utility, or pleasure, or the highest things, that is, the contemplation of truth. There is nothing wrong with any of these in principle. Friendship always softens the harshness of justice, which looks not to the person but to the equity of the relationship. Friendship's essence is reciprocity. That is, it is the mutual regard of the good in another and a wish for that good to be what it is. It is not self-centered but other-centered.

Aristotle rightly thought that cities were more dependent on friendship than on justice. But this did not mean that he thought that everyone could be friends with everyone else or that justice was unimportant. Quite the opposite.

He saw that the number of good friends based on the highest virtues was few. This is not a bad thing, though it does create a problem that revelation addresses. In this life, we must acknowledge as a fact that it takes a lifetime to know someone else fully. A good society in this world, at least, would not be one in which everyone was a friend of everyone else, as Plato sometimes thought, but a society containing a multiplicity of friends, few of whom had more than a few good friends, but where all were friendly or considerate of others.

Friends, however, have need of something to be friends about. The highest activity of the human being, that in which his natural happiness consists, is the contemplation of the truth, that is, of knowing the order of things, what life and the world and their sources are about. How much of this we can know is not infinite, but we seek to know what we can. We realize that we have an infinite desire to know *all that is*. Thus, the highest acts of friendship are the exchanges of knowledge and benevolence that seek to know the truth and, in diverse ways, to incorporate the good and the beautiful into our lives. The knowledge of the truth is not conceived as unrelated to the practical life, but is rather seen as its inspiration.

We can and should speak of two kinds of happiness. One is the kind of happiness that we can experience and describe for a mortal being while he is alive in this world. This kind of happiness consists in acquiring and practicing the virtues in a proper order. The second kind of happiness seems to open out into a world whose completion is difficult to discern by the human mind. It is traditionally called "contemplative happiness". This completion is what we should strive for insofar as we can.

Aristotle calls contemplative happiness the activity of the highest faculty on the highest object in a complete life. As with Plato, it brings us face-to-face with the question of our immortality and our final destiny in the universe. What we can know of the highest things, we should strive to know. The proper order of soul includes the effort and discipline to know the meaning of things, including human things. It also includes the exchanges with our friends about these things, about the world we live in and the lives we lead.

The contemplation of the highest things is not, or ought not to be, a closed enterprise. It is the opening of the mind on what the world can tell us about itself. Contemplation is also something that is capable of listening to answers to its own questions, questions whose answers it knows are insufficiently answered by the human mind itself. This fact that the human mind does not supply all answers to its own questions can be a cause of despair, or an opening to other answers proposed to it that have sufficient evidence to be taken seriously.

The order of the soul means, in the end, that we are finite beings in the understanding of our own powers and being, but within that finiteness, we have been given a contemplative power that seems to be open to what is more than human. We do want to consider the things of the greatest value, as Plato said. Our final happiness is not achieved by escaping to someplace else. It is a question of what is in us, what we are. With Johnson, we do well to be aware of the difficulty of coming to know well what is true. But with Aristotle, we must acknowledge that it is worthwhile making the effort. We can know some things as true. The effort to know such things seems to be what the order of the soul, including its own order, is about.

CHAPTER V

THE ORDER OF POLITY

> This is the principle which a wise man must follow in his relations towards his own city. Let him warn her, if he thinks her constitution is corrupt and there is a prospect that his words will be listened to and not put him in danger of his life; but let him not use violence upon his fatherland to bring about a change of constitution. If what he thinks is best can only be accomplished by the exile and slaughter of men, let him keep his peace and pray for the welfare of himself and his city.
>
> —Plato *Seventh Letter* 331d

> For, if the diverse agents that cause the diversity of things are ordered to one another, there must be some single cause of this order; for many things are not united save by some one thing. And thus the ordering principle of this unity is the first and sole cause of the distinction of things.
>
> —Thomas Aquinas, *Summa contra Gentiles*, 2, 41

I

The order of polity is directly related to the order of the souls of its members, its citizens. Polity expresses an intelligible human order and depends on it, while at the same time it makes this order fully possible. This is why there is no orderly city without a knowledge and practice of orderly souls. The composition of any polity includes the moral condition of the souls of its members. In this sense, what is private is also public, as what is public ultimately originates in and flows from what is internal, or private. It is not possible to know a city without knowing the virtues and vices, in their variety, of those who inhabit it. There will always be a range of virtue and vice in every city, the differing mixtures of which will be part of what differentiates cities or polities one from another, in their moral if not their legal forms.

The polity is not a single being or substantial organism, as are individual human persons or other living beings. Understanding this distinction, we can see why individual persons are ultimately more real, more important than polities. Polities, unlike the individual persons, have no transcendent destiny beyond their accidental reality, itself dependent on the existence of human persons in which this accidental reality inheres. The polity is an association or arrangement of citizens who will or choose to live together for the purpose both of living and of living well. They are bound together, or bind themselves together, by law, custom, and friendship. Their actions, following the laws and customs, are the means of achieving a chosen good.

Aristotle insisted in his *Politics* in including the family as a necessary institution in which human beings normally live. Polity is not opposed to family, but demands it. A family begins with the marriage of a man and a woman in a permanent life for the relation of spouses and the begetting of children. This is the primary need of every child—that it be begotten and raised in a family in which the generosity and identity of actual parents are recognized. No institution can replace the family, and the family's breakup or dissolution will ever be a major factor in undermining any polity. It is in the family wherein the main habits and virtues are initially learned and practiced. Each family is intended to produce children who grow and produce other families, who at maturity enter the polity.

The polity is the relation of order that exists among citizens who act according to (or sometimes against) the rules or laws established in the city. The law identifies the mode of proceeding in the relation of citizens to one another, including their relation to their own rulers, as well as to citizens of other polities. Individual citizens bear the reality of *what is*. But individual citizens are constantly coming into the polity through birth or immigration and passing out of it through death, exile, or emigration. The coming into being, the passing out of being, the sustenance in being is primarily found in the intermediate institution of the family. In its relation to the inculcation and carrying out of virtue and vice, the family is also of fundamental importance.

The "reality" of a polity lies in the categories of action, passion, and relation, not substance. A polity thus cannot "save its soul" or bear a collective guilt or praise apart from actual individual persons, in their chosen actions, who make up the polity in the past, present, and future. A polity, as an order of relations, is intended to outlast the lives of its individual members so that generations of the same family can live in the same polity. But the polity is not a "thing", apart from existing citizens, claiming its own substantial life.

In the context of world politics, significantly differing polities will be found that, over the centuries, come into being and cease to exist for various reasons, usually internal moral decay or conquest from outside. Generally, polities, in their history, need at some point to defend themselves to remain what they are. Civil wars and strife can also radically change the form of polities almost beyond recognition, something clearly taught by the great Thucydides. Polities, as we just mentioned, are intended to be "immortal", that is, to continue on down the ages, beyond the limits of an individual lifetime. But few polities ever last more than several centuries in their original forms. World history records many polities, like many plant and animal species, that have ceased to exist. Moreover, there are many nations or peoples who would desire to form their own separate polities but are prevented by force or ability properly to organize themselves into independent polities.

II

The different forms of politics are classified as monarchies (rule of one wise), aristocracies (rule of few virtuous), and "polities" (rule of the many of ordinary virtues). These are good forms. Their corresponding bad forms are tyranny (rule of one disordered man), oligarchy (rule of few, usually rich), and democracy (rule of many who do not have ordered souls). Mixed regimes are a combination of these simpler forms. This is the classical classification, each of which category, as we will see, has its own intelligibility and configuration. In the modern era, almost every polity, even the worst, seeks to define itself as a republic or a democracy. This tendency necessitates a twofold endeavor to distinguish between (a) what the regime or polity claims it is and (b) what it actually is in terms of its operative philosophic purpose and organization. Thus, it is possible to speak of a "democratic tyranny" when the end of the polity, even if under the guidance of popular rule, acts for tyrannical purposes. Likewise, apparent monarchies in practice may well act as republics.

These forms of regime define the location of the ruling or deciding principle of the polity and usually its general end or purpose. In this sense, the polity agrees about the authority, that is, who makes the final decisions about common and binding laws, whether that authority be one, a few, or many citizens. All good forms of polity rule for a common good. All bad forms rule for the good of the ruling principle, however it is defined. Thus, a monarchy is the rule of one good man, or ruler, for the good of all. It has the advantage of unity or certainty of judgment of the ruling principle both for what goes right and for what goes wrong. An oligarchy is the rule of a few, usually the rich, for the preservation and fostering of wealth as the principal end of human action. In understanding a polity, it is important accurately to see its real constitution, or to observe by what principles it lives and governs itself. The accurate definition or designation of a polity's form is one of the most difficult and dangerous of enterprises of practical reasoning and politics. Very few corrupt or disordered regimes will admit, or allow others to admit, their objective condition. They will often threaten or eliminate those who seek to point it out.

"Man is by nature a political animal" is the famous statement of Aristotle about the full manifestation and completion of human nature among human beings actually living in this world. By themselves, men are not fully what they are or are intended to be, a fact that does not indicate that there is something wrong with them, only something that needs to be realized. Man's political nature includes and presupposes his rational and domestic nature. The rational and domestic aspect of a single human nature is not, in principle, to be seen in conflict with its city-living nature. To be a political being means that the goods available to man for his living and prospering are expanded and perfected by his living in a polity. This polity is formed by a proper law or constitution, which may be either written or customary. The fact that there are many differing polities is itself a natural and good thing both because there are differing ways to achieve real goods and because the opportunity for as many as possible to act politically is itself a good.

The polity includes a common good that makes possible the many particular and corporate goods coming into being through human intelligence and enterprise. The "common good" is not some good existing beyond the goods within the polity. It is the good that the polity concretely produces. It includes the idea that there are human goods, including those of the family, and transcendent ones. It is a good that includes the goods of individual, familial, and social life that it makes possible. The common good is the good that enables many other goods to be possible.

When we say that man is by "nature" a political animal, we are in effect looking at one aspect of what it means for man to be "rational". It is reasonable to associate with others to accomplish things, including moral, intellectual, and artistic things, that would otherwise remain unfinished or impossible without the organized relation to others. The polity is, at its best, also to proceed by reason and persuasion to reach its own goals. The fact that the polity also has to use coercion or violence, themselves beyond reason though not contrary to it when used to prevent evils, is not a "natural" part of the essence of a polity but exists only on the supposition that some citizens act unreasonably.

Man would, in fact, be political even if there were no need for coercion or force. But the use of force itself, by authority of the polity, is or should also be a reasonable activity in the circumstances. Generally, the need for the wise use of force, be it police or army, will always be present. Notions that it can be completely eliminated are utopian and dangerous. The wise understanding and use of force is itself a fundamental part of the common good. Force represents a failure of reason and virtue. But it also indicates real problems that constantly must be dealt with in an orderly fashion by the polity.

At first sight, of course, the order of polity will seem primarily to concern force. In fact, many ancient and modern theories of politics maintain that the only order possible in politics—we think of Hobbes—is that resulting from force. Here, we argue, rather, that force is a factor that follows from the need to deal with a lack of a proper order in our souls. It is to be legitimately used only in the name of ordered reason. Empirically, we usually note the presence of government in any polity when we see the police, or the soldier, or the magistrate, or the tax collector. Each of these officers or legal offices represents an effort to keep order within the polity against those forces that would cause disorder. It is reasonable that force used for order exist even if it is unfortunate that it has to exist among imperfect beings.

Force and violence bring up the question of the kind of beings of which the polity is composed. Obviously, it is not composed wholly of perfect beings who never act unreasonably or selfishly. A failure to understand this unsettling dimension of man, including other indications of his fallen nature, will lead to either too much or too little reliance on coercion. In this sense, our political institutions are themselves related to our political philosophy and its own understanding of its normal human problems. These institutions in turn reflect the souls of those who inhabit the polity. Though it is not the essence of politics, coercion and its relation to disorder are elements in every polity that need themselves to be dealt with in a reasonable manner. It is not a defect that man contains emotions and passions beyond reason, even when they can and should be ruled by reason. Politics presupposes our understanding of the internal order or disorder of human beings. Without this knowledge, we would not know that which is to be ruled in a polity.

III

To understand the order of polity, the first thing we need to appreciate, as Aristotle put it, is that there are two kinds of happiness, one properly called "political" and one called "theoretical" or "speculative". Both kinds of happiness are directly pertinent to the sort of being we are, and both forms of happiness are related to each other. Each human being is ordained to both and, for a complete life, needs to experience both. Political happiness is its own natural good, while at the same time it is ordered to the good of contemplation. Contemplation itself is ordered to what is ultimately worth contemplating, for its own sake. Political happiness refers to the good function of man with regard to his own virtues and with regard to these virtues in relation to others. It refers to the full blossoming, inasmuch as that is possible, of the human being in all his mortal potential.

At first sight, this distinction between political and theoretical happiness might sound unnecessary or confusing. But it contains an important point that is necessary to understand to prevent politics from being something other than it is. We do not want politics claiming to provide a transcendent happiness that is beyond its nature. It is this distinction between political and contemplative happiness, moreover, that is important for revelation's relation to politics. In one sense, we can say that revelation deals both with politics as a practical science or as a temporal happiness and also with a transcendent good that in no wise is directly political.

Thus we find admonitions in revelation both to worship God alone and to give our neighbor in need a cup of water. These are sometimes very lofty, very difficult, and very particular admonitions. They indicate that man's life in the polity, wherein a drink of water might be needed, is never sufficient to satisfy his inner and objective longings that are insufficiently satisfied in the political order in this world. Indeed, the need for a cup of water hints that the polity itself is often not sufficient even for its own purposes and depends on motivations that are often beyond politics.

It seems, in other words, that we need a defense both of the legitimacy of polities in a proper limited form wherein human beings can be what they are and of the thesis that politics does not exhaust the individual person's meaning or purpose. This reflection takes us back to the earlier comment that man is a political animal but also something more. The polity is not itself the basis of being and action but merely a relation among acting persons who are achieving purposes both political and more than political. Political happiness does not mean that some separate "being" called the polity (the Leviathan) is happy. It means, rather, that human persons, who compose any polity, are relatively better off—happier—because they are organized in a political way. In this manner, they can experience and acquire goods, including goods of intellect, beauty, and worthiness, that would be impossible without it.

But even when the polity exists and flourishes, it does not provide everything needed for human happiness even in this world. Man was not created simply for this world. The polity thus can conceivably be completely successful in its own order and still be filled with citizens who are not completely happy or fulfilled in a more complete sense. Indeed, this condition will always be the case. This realization is itself sufficient to alert us to the fact that man, while being a political animal, is more than a political animal. Man's highest function, his contemplative activity, is not, as such, political. His highest natural function in this world while in this world, doing the things of this world, is, however, political. In other words, what is political, by being itself, can, and should, make what is more than political to be possible and indeed to flourish. That is, the good political order enables man to have the leisure to concentrate on *what is*, on what is more than political, on reality itself.

What, then, is political happiness? Obviously, if man is by nature a political being, to be a member of and a participant in the political life of a polity will be something contributory to the happiness in this mortal life of what it is to be a human being. Man is to use his mind in those ways available to him, including the kind of ruling that requires mind and persuasion in the polity. In the history of political thought and institutions, however, often the noblest human beings, say, Socrates or Christ, have been seen as fulfilling their highest human purpose over against the polity.

Indeed, the trials of Socrates and Christ themselves serve to indicate the limits of politics. Had either Socrates or Christ agreed to save his life by denying some higher good for which he stood in order to follow a disorder of politics, all of political philosophy would have been different. Their deaths, their refusals to do wrong at the behest of the polity, served to focus attention on the fundamental question of whether happiness was ultimately only political. That is, their deaths affirmed that there is a "polity" in which they would not have been killed, the city in speech, the City of God. Contemplative happiness itself, for which both stood, was something more than political.

Yet these more transcendent questions that are directly related to actual polities are not intended to deny the importance or significance of actual polities, even if they are not the final location of human happiness. The best things are not necessarily opposed to the second- or third-best things. In fact, the lesser goods are themselves necessary or important to the higher things, as the scriptural example of giving a cup of water indicates. And it is on this principle that we can describe the order or orders of polity as contributing to a proper human happiness that itself is not the final happiness to which each human being is ordered. Any actual polity can choose to oppose such ultimate happiness. Polities in history have opposed truth and goodness. But it need not be this way. One might even say that there is a certain poignancy in good and peaceful regimes that do all they can to foster the human good but find in the end that they are not the final instruments to supply it.

In a famous passage in his *Politics*, Aristotle examined the best regimes that were proposed by earlier philosophers. He directly referred to Plato in his *Republic*. Aristotle thought in that book that Plato's Socrates sought too much unity for his best regime. Aristotle went on to suggest that the polity, while it has a certain unity of order, does not want to be unified as a human substance. The good of the polity is precisely not to be overly unified, so that the many goods that might exist can actually come to pass. In order for the whole to be the whole, the parts must be, and remain, the parts. It is on this principle that we see that the polity is an order of many parts that are good to exist. We do not necessarily know ahead of time how many there will be or what they will look like, as these need to be fashioned. But the polity exists that the parts may appear and accomplish things that would not otherwise be possible. Here, "parts" refers to human persons both individually and organized into families or other associations, each looking to a proper and possible good.

A polity, moreover, will not simply come about or hold together by itself. It must be caused to be what it is, to become and remain a unity among different goods. And this cause is something active, something practical. It is addressed to this particular polity in its own configuration. What the polity needs to accomplish this unity among many parts is an authority or ruling principle itself devoted to this end or purpose. When Aristotle said that man is "by nature a political animal", he meant both that man's perfection requires a polity and that it was necessary for this polity to be itself set up and carried on by human enterprise and reason. The polity was "natural", not in the sense that it grew from a seed, but in that it was reasonable as an institution in which human goods and human safety could flourish. In other words, just as the individual human being needs to rule or guide with reason those things in himself that require guidance toward his end, principally his passions and relationship with others, so too a polity needs an active reason guiding it to its own temporal purpose, whereby the parts can function as they are but in a way that is ordered to or limited by the broader needs of the whole.

In one sense, the forms of government that were mentioned—monarchy, aristocracy, polity / democracy, oligarchy, and tyranny—are but ways to designate the ruling principle or authority established in this or that regime. The authority is that source or body—it may itself be complex—in which binding laws are proposed, established, and enforced. The purpose of this authority is not itself or its own good, but the good of the order of the whole.

The best way to clarify what is at issue is Aquinas' famous definition of law as "an ordination of reason for the common good promulgated by the proper authority". Notice that this definition of law does not directly include coercion or force, as if to say that the essence of law is reason and persuasion. Coercion arises only when persuasion fails. If someone obeys a law because he sees it is reasonable to do so, he is not coerced. He is acting reasonably.

Thus the essence or form of the law is reason, the reason that went to make this law to be what it is. Law is an appeal of mind to mind, the mind of the lawgiver to the mind of the one who obeys the law, so that both can act reasonably in their relations in the polity. It is clear that political decisions must be made in order that a community can continue and prosper. Moreover, there are always many good alternatives open to lawgivers from among which to choose what is to be done. The choice is not always, or even usually, between good and evil but between good and less good laws. Some selection needs to be made since not all alternatives can go into effect at once. This selection of what is to be binding law is the function of the authority as properly set up and operative in a given polity. The purpose of the law, in good regimes, is not the good of the lawmaking body, but the general good of the citizens.

Once a law is agreed upon, it can of course be changed if it does not work, though easy or frequent changing of laws usually militates against good political order. But normally, observance of laws has to do with habit and getting used to obeying them. Once they are in effect, they establish the way citizens relate to one another. It is possible to have good written laws and corrupt citizens, or, as Edmund Burke pointed out, to have bad laws and good citizens who manage to modify the badness of the law by custom. The order of polity is, at its basic level, an order of laws designed to facilitate the common good of the citizens.

The promulgation of laws is designed to emphasize that laws need to be understood by the citizens and agreed to at least implicitly as the proper way of acting in a particular polity. Promulgation means making known what is to be done by those who are obliged by the law in question. To explain law to people who can understand what it means is an act of political freedom. Obedience to law is not an imposition on the human mind from outside, even if the one who obeys the law does not make it. Rather, obedience is the acknowledgment on the part of the citizen that the law is worthy of obedience, even if it is not the abstractly "best" law or even if other laws might have been selected. The law is thus a proposal of practical reason to citizens who want to act rationally in their relations to others. They seek to know in a particular case how to do this. Generally, they know that doing things according to the law is good.

Laws, as we have indicated, can be changed by a reasonable process, itself usually set up by law or modified by custom. The heart of a law is the reason embodied in its formulation. It is the reason of the authority in its defined configuration that is operative to decide what is to be done. The law is not to be designed for any private good of the lawgivers or faction of the citizens, but for the common good. And the law needs to be understood by the citizens so that the polity can exist in persuasion, not primarily coercion. This does not mean that sanctions are unnecessary, though they should largely be so. A society whose order is mostly established and carried on by force, not persuasion, is a very dangerous and weak one. The sanctions of the law are themselves part of the reasonableness of the law and indicate the seriousness or importance of the law. A law that bears a small fine for its breaking is not of the same importance as one that has, say, life imprisonment or death attached to its violation.

Inherent in this discussion of the order of polity as established by decisions of legitimate authority for a common good is the fact that laws do bind us in our conscience if they are reasonable. They are reasonable if they contain the four elements of reason, common good, legitimate authority, and promulgation. If they do not, they are not true laws and do not bind us to obey them except perhaps in prudence. No one can be obliged to observe an immoral law, though he can be forced to do so. The world is more full of those who have been eliminated for refusing to obey immoral laws than we are at first sight wont to admit. The examples of Socrates and Christ remain here the abiding lessons of political order, both that it is limited to what is reasonable and that men have a destiny that transcends the political order. When this order places itself between the human being and his end, it violates the most precious purpose of its own existence, the common good of persons who have both a political and a transcendent destiny.

IV

Aristotle had remarked that even though justice was the virtue that was most visible in the polity, still justice was of less importance than friendship, even to the polity itself. This is a remarkable observation and already points to things beyond politics as most central to human living. Yet, if we return to the goods that are most central to human happiness, both political and theoretical goods, it is clear that friendship of citizens one with another is crucial for modifying the harshness of justice, which, to be sure, is a virtue. There has long been an illusion that citizens on a vast scale, thousands and millions of them, could be friends at the highest levels, and if not, there is something wrong with the polity. But this universal friendship is not possible in any practical sense. Friends of everybody are friends of nobody, as an old saying goes. We cannot have more than a few good friends in this life. The order of polity thus ought to foster, not hinder, those institutions, especially the family, in which friendship and what is beyond justice have their regular and highest expressions.

Thus, it is important properly to understand the relation of friendship to polity. In general, as we remarked in the previous chapter, the best form of common good is not one in which everyone is a friend with everyone else, though a general friendliness is possible, something called "concord" by the classical authors. This would be the weakest kind of friendship, but an improvement over bare justice. But concord is not the kind of friendship in which the highest things can easily exist. The highest friendships take a lifetime to complete. It is quite true and good that we have more friendships based on utility or pleasure. Again, these modify and soften human relationships and are sometimes the origin of deeper friendships. We should not hide the paradox that this natural contrast between polity and friendship brings up. Since justice to all and friendship to a few are both goods of a high order, we must conceive an order of polity in which both can exist and flourish.

The structural problem of political life would evidently require a polity in which citizens could participate in the decision and judging function of a polity both as an exercise of their own virtue and as a contribution to the common good. This political form would make possible the exercise of practical reason at the political level. At the same time, all citizens would recognize that, though it is a high good, political participation at its best is not the highest end for which man is fashioned. Thus, he still should be free and encouraged to pursue things that are either not political—economic things, for instance—or beyond politics.

But this pursuit could be possible only if the political order were itself philosophically open and well organized enough to allow it. The common good that is made possible by the order of polity includes but does not define the friendships that freely come about among individual persons in any decent polity. In a sense, this friendship is what the polity is for, not that it creates them but that it allows friendships to happen. It does this by making it possible through security of law and, indeed, prosperity. Friendship requires the virtue of liberality, in which one's property can be used for higher human goods.

Again, we are reminded that bad as well as good regimes occur. One of the characteristics of the worst regime (tyranny) is its positive effort to make friendship, especially friendship of the highest kind, impossible. It does this by forcing everything to be public, by preventing any kind of work but public work, by keeping the citizens occupied in building monuments or in war, by striving to know everything that happens. This tyrannical effort is designed to prevent plots against the regime. It is recognized that friendships of good men are the most likely sources of opposition to bad rule.

This consideration serves to remind us that while there are things that transcend politics, it remains true that politics can, if not properly organized, serve to deflect or deform the human good. When this happens, it becomes of primary importance that bad regimes be changed. The distinction between political and contemplative happiness is not designed to make the good citizen unaware of or indifferent to disorders of regime. Disordered regimes are themselves threats against the possibility of achieving the highest human goods. They need to be understood and dealt with.

The problem of deformed political regimes itself thus requires a major theoretical endeavor to understand. The analysis of disordered polities is, indeed, an essential aspect of political philosophy. So important is the proper understanding of the place of politics in the order of things, that we can argue that the major alternative to God in the modern world can be conceived, and often has been conceived, as a political order. Such an order claims complete independence of any natural or divine influence in its judgment about what is to be done in the political order, which looks to nothing higher than itself.

This deformed regime then claims to be able by itself to make men happy in this world, which, in its own way, is itself a divine claim. Aristotle had already noticed that if man were the highest being in the universe, politics would in fact be the highest science. Since man is not the highest being, politics is limited. That is, politics cannot claim to be the institution in which the ultimate human goods are defined or achieved, though it can be the institution that allows men to seek and pursue these goals in the proper way they can be achieved.

But in maintaining that the polity is limited, it is not necessary to deny that it is a central institution in which very important goods are to be achieved and are worthy of being achieved. This is why the order of polity is itself a legitimate subject of human inquiry. And it is largely when the polity is what it is supposed to be by nature that the higher things can come into being for most people most of the time. This is the general good that justifies all good polities.

"Political realism" has been a common term used to address the fact that most polities most of the time and most citizens within them are not perfect. Human beings are fallible and finite, but still good and worthy of existence. Sometimes, as with Machiavelli, "realism" was simply a denial of any moral standards except success. Staying in power justified the means of doing so. But more generally, in this view, realism meant that since we cannot obtain everything we want, we have to lessen our expectations. Sometimes it was better to allow imperfect or even evil practices if we could not immediately correct them without causing greater harm. Those who wanted too much, especially too much perfection, often were the most dangerous threats to a reasonable and practical common good.

Throughout history, in fact, most actual regimes—mostly tyrannies, oligarchies, and democracies—were less than perfect, regimes that in principle looked to the good of the ruling principle and not to the good of the whole. This meant that those who understood the disorder of the polity had to learn to live within it in such a way as to survive and, if possible, work to correct it. The problem of tyranny, and its more extreme modern form, totalitarianism, has necessitated both an empirical and theoretical analysis as to its meaning and incidence. Understanding in what ways bad regimes deviate from good regimes is itself a worthy exercise in political thought and a step to improving any order of polity.

V

In this light, revelation can be seen in one sense as a response to the fact that most men, most of the time in history, have lived in imperfect regimes. They did not in their lives achieve anything like the political happiness of which we spoke as the purpose of the polity. If we are going to speak of their "happiness", we cannot do so in terms of the actual regime in which they lived other than in the sense that they transcended it by living good lives, even within corrupt regimes. The transcendent good is not closed to those in terrible regimes. This is what the order of redemption is about (chapter 8).

This achieving a higher end was often possible in corrupt regimes, even if not widespread or easy. Gulags and concentration camps produced more than their share of saints. Not infrequently, life in a disordered polity led to martyrdom or a life of suffering. But this conflict reminds us again of the very nature of the order of polity, that it stands under a higher order that limits it. The polity can either contribute to or hinder this higher order, but it cannot eliminate it even when it kills, say, Socrates or Christ, or even any ordinary citizen.

If we could propose the best form of polity that is reasonable to describe or expect in this life, what would it be like? Philosophers have often claimed that the issue of the best regime is at the heart of political philosophy. To discuss the best regime means that we can define and analyze the less-than-best regimes in its comparative light. We can state how we ought to live even if we do not live this way ourselves. Again, the cycle of regimes is related to the order of soul of the citizens who make it up. What needs to be established here is that the best regime, the one that would be most conducive to most human beings most of the time, will not be a regime in which, by its own methods, all human problems are solved or in which all human aspirations are fulfilled. Rather, it is more likely to be a regime in which the most perplexing human problems are allowed to be addressed in institutions such as families, universities, churches, or associations, wherein the proper atmosphere for addressing them is promoted and protected.

Ever since Plato and Augustine, we are familiar with the fact that the highest life is presented in political terms. Obviously, this association is intelligible because man's social nature, together with the trinitarian nature of the Godhead, suggests that friendship, communion, and love are at the heart of the highest things. The best practical political regime for men while they are active and present in this world would not itself be the locus in which the highest things exist. But it would not be set up against these goals and the institutions in which they flourish. It would, indeed, contribute to their possibility. Since the political life is itself a real good and one that in some sense is required for the happiness of man in this world, we can speak of the best regime as something feasible and worthy of human endeavor. This is a moderate understanding of political life, one that better conforms to the actual condition of actual people in most regimes.

Aristotle thought the best regime was a monarchy. He was thinking of the unity of authority necessary to make decisions. The single monarch, whether hereditary or elected, has the advantage of clarity of decision. If the ruling principle is multiple, as in an aristocracy or polity, it is generally the case that decisions will not be unanimous. They will be less clear and persuasive. This division of ruling principle means that the actual law will appear weak because there are members of the ruling body who do not agree with the choice of law, even when they agree to abide by it. Suppose in an aristocracy, the rule of the virtuous, that the decision-making power is in the hands of a body of thirteen. In this case the votes of seven would rule. The dissenting votes of six would indicate that this decision or law is not clear, as there were arguments against it. The same would be true in polity. Close votes indicate weakness, not strength or certainty, of decision.

On the other hand, a good practical regime should contain opportunities for the many actually to exercise prudential choice in ruling, however this is configured into the constitution. In this sense, the best regime would be popular, recognizing talent and prudence and gradually allowing many citizens to participate in the "to rule" of the society. The best practical regime would insist that the rulers be in some sense accountable to the ruled, who would themselves be internally ordered enough to judge well the quality of their rulers and their proposals.

But the best regime would also be based on the dignity of each person. It would recognize the political nature of each citizen as well as the transcendent destiny on which this dignity is based. Normally, this aspect of the best regime is spoken of in terms of "rights", but this concept has certain confusions connected with it. In modern political theory, the term "rights" does not refer to an objective description of what man is, but rather to whatever it is he wills for himself. It is an idea primarily associated with Hobbes and can, in the form of "willed rights", undermine any objective order of polity. One can speak of human duties, rather than rights, to make the point that there is an objective order that is worth serving, not because its content is made up by our own wills, but because a true good is found in human life that is worth achieving.

Like the word "rights", the word "democracy" also has a troubled meaning, though it is the word that most often serves to describe the best practical regime among modern writers and politicians. The Greek word, from which the modern word is taken, means the rule of the many, but of the many who are not virtuous. These are the many who implicitly define their end and the end of the regime as "freedom" or "liberty", wherein "liberty" means not the ordered pursuit of good and truth, but doing whatever it is we want. Thus, democracy in the classical sense has no criterion of the good other than what one wills to call good. In this sense, democracy, based on a relativist or sceptical view of reality, undermines any proper order of polity. The accurate definition and understanding of political words is thus of great importance in preserving or improving a polity.

Normally, we would like to say that the best regime is one that conceives itself as limited to the temporal common good—that it protects "rights", that it is based on a free market, that it is checked by and participated in by its own citizens, and finally that it is open to truth as an objective reality. This is what is often called "democracy", and the word can be used if the proper distinctions about its content are made. If we can accept this understanding of the best regime, we can recommend that it ought to be the regime of choice among the nations. The realist view does not deny that there are likely to be many disordered regimes.

Some think it is wrong or dangerous to try to change disordered regimes, especially by utopian schemes to change man by changing his polity. On the other hand, if the disordered regimes are repressive and dangerous both to their own citizens and to other peoples, it does seem that efforts both within a polity and from the outside to change the regime are also part of the enterprise of the order of polity. This need not be a formula to identify all regimes as needing change. But it is an acknowledgment that some regimes are better than others and that disordered regimes are dangerous both to their citizens and to others.

We can conclude the reflection on the order of polity by recalling the universality of propositions such as those found in the Declaration of Independence. Certain truths are self-evident. Political actions of the nations need to be presented to the nations for judgment on the basis of some objective and intelligible criterion that all admit. The famous passage from the Gettysburg Address about a government of the people, for the people, and by the people is not just the possession of one nation. It is a criterion for all nations about the best order of polity. It is something that can be grasped only if we also understand the order of our souls and the order of family. In the regime under which we live, we seek the limited good which polities are designed to establish. That there is a good that is beyond politics is itself a truth implicit in the very notion of what is a polity.

CHAPTER VI

THE ORDER OF MIND

> The practical construction of an objective world, the manipulation of inorganic nature, is the confirmation of man as a conscious species-being, i.e. a being who treats the species as his own being or himself as a species-being.
>
> —Karl Marx[1]

> As a distinct science, [logic] is primarily concerned with the formal aspect of thought, not with the nature or origin of our concepts, and still less with the existence and nature of these external objects. If you ask logic to answer a philosophical question, you can expect but a logical answer, not a philosophical one, with the unavoidable consequence that your question will appear as unanswerable, and as a pseudo-question.
>
> —Étienne Gilson[2]

I

During a sailing race of clipper ships across the North Atlantic from New York Harbor to Lizard Point at the tip of

[1] Eric Fromm, *Marx's Concept of Man*, with a translation from Marx' "Alienated Labor", from Karl Marx, *Economic and Philosophic Manuscripts of 1844*, trans. T.B. Bottomore (New York: Ungar, 1961), 1:23, 102.

[2] Étienne Gilson, "Logicism and Philosophy", in *The Unity of Philosophical Experience* (San Francisco: Ignatius Press, [1937] 1999), 10.

England during June 2005, Angus Phillips wrote a series of accounts of various aspects of the voyage. He is the *Washington Post* "outdoors" reporter and a voluntary crewman on the *Stadt Amsterdam*, a huge, well-equipped clipper ship taking part in the race. Phillips recounted that the oldest member of the crew, a man eighty-three years old by the name of Bruce Lockwood, claims to have been in over eight thousand races since 1926.

However, Lockwood's most memorable claim to fame was of another order. In his past, he had, three days in a row, rescued the famed scientist Albert Einstein from a capsized dinghy in the choppy waters of Peconic Bay, Long Island. In recounting these scenes, Lockwood remarked of Einstein's recurring inability to control the dinghy: "He didn't have common sense. His mind just didn't work like yours and mine." Phillips adds another story of the great scientist. "Einstein was also said to be so poor a piano player, his teacher once threw up his hands in despair, blurting out, 'Albert, you can't count!'"[3] The abilities to count and control dinghies are, of course, among the ordinary accomplishments of ordinary men using their ordinary minds to deal with the ordinary world before them.

Such amusing instances serve to alert us to the differences in orders, to different kinds of knowledge—practical and theoretical, scientific and musical. If we do not have practical order, as evident in the case of Einstein and sailboating, it does not follow that we do not have another kind of order. We may understand scientific order but not nautical order. A place for common sense must remain in the world, just to keep us afloat. Our minds work fine once

[3] Angus Phillips, "Hearing the Bells That Toll Crossing the North Atlantic", *The Washington Post*, June 1, 2005.

we know or learn the proper order. We do want, ultimately, to know how normal minds, yours and mine, work. A man can be a genius in one order and a veritable klutz in another. It happens all the time, not infrequently in ourselves. It is part of the human condition of having to learn how to do or understand different sorts of activities. And we admittedly find geniuses who understand things most of us do not.

Two of the four categories of order that Aquinas specifically mentions in the prologue to his commentary on Aristotle's *Ethics*—the order of things we do not make but consider, and the order of the voluntary things we put in our actions either by ourselves or with others—have been considered. The order of things we make will be treated in chapter 9 under the aspect of beauty. To skipper a sailboat, to know its order, is a matter of practical intellect, an art or skill that requires learning and practice. To these orders, I have added a consideration of the ordered internal life of the Godhead. The order of hell and the order of redemption, orders that relate also to revelation, will be found in chapters 7 and 8.

Here we will touch upon the fourth order that Aquinas mentions, namely, the order that "reason, in considering, establishes in its own act; for example, when it arranges its concepts among themselves and the signs of concepts, since they are sounds that signify something." I do not intend to present a course in minor logic here, though that is a worthy study at this point.[4] The point of logic and principle was well made by Chesterton: "Yet a truth is equally solemn

[4] See, for example, Paul Tidman and Howard Kahane, *Logic and Philosophy* (Belmont, Calif.: Thompson/Wadsworth, 2003); Harry J. Gansler, *Introduction to Logic* (London: Routledge, 2001).

whatever figure or example its exponent adopts. It is an equally awful truth that four and four make eight, whether you reckon the thing out in eight onions or eight angels, or eight bricks or eight bishops, or eight minor poets or eight pigs."[5] Such a passage is not merely a lesson in mathematics, but also one in induction and logic, even metaphysics. The examples point to the essence, and the essence abstracts from the examples. The order of the mind's own tools of thinking is an important topic.

I will add something on the art of rhetoric, the art of persuasion, since it too has to do with the importance of logical argument and opinion. Aristotle had already made this connection in the very first lines of his *Posterior Analytics*, where he deals with logical matters. "All instruction given or received by way of argument proceeds from pre-existing knowledge", Aristotle writes.

> This becomes evident upon a survey of all the species of such instruction. The mathematical sciences and all other speculative disciplines are acquired in this way, and so are the two forms of dialectical reasoning, syllogism and induction, for each of these latter makes use of old knowledge to impart new, the syllogism assuming an audience that accepts its premises, induction exhibiting the universal as implicit in the clearly known particular. Again, the persuasion exerted by rhetorical arguments is in principle the same, since they are either example, a kind of induction, or enthymeme, a form of syllogism.[6] (71a1–10)

[5] G.K. Chesterton, "Spiritualism", in *All Things Considered* (New York: Sheed and Ward, 1956), 148.

[6] "Enthymeme" is a technical Greek word that literally means "to keep in mind". Technically, it is a syllogism in which one of the premises is implicit, that is, known or assumed by everyone in the audience. "We cannot trust this man, for he has lied in the past" is an enthymeme, a

Both to know the argument for the truth of a thing and to be persuaded to accept the truth of some open position are based on a logical order of principles.

To introduce this topic, however, I have cited what, at first sight, might seem like peculiar, even obscure, passages from both Karl Marx, the founder of communism, and Étienne Gilson, the great Thomist historian of philosophy. Indeed, I cite Marx as an example of the problem that Gilson was pointing out, namely, that logic, as such, has nothing to do with the existence or nature of external objects.

"Purely intellectual activity", Mortimer Adler wrote, "cannot occur without some activity of the sensitive powers, but the content of conceptual thought is not affected by it. We can think conceptually of that which is not sensible at all, and not imaginable."[7] We never encounter the "idea" of a dog walking down the street, only particular dogs from whom we eventually derive the idea of what a dog is or what walking is. The idea of dog abstracts from all individual dogs. We can think about dogs even if no dogs are around us at the time, though we do need to remember what they are. This idea—dog, say—as universal exists only in our mind, but it is a real knowledge derived from reality. Logic thus could conceivably exist if nothing else but mind existed, even though Aristotle's logic, the one that is still the most basic discussion of the topic, is itself designed as an aid in the proper knowing of real things. It begins with real things, not logical abstractions.

---

truncated syllogism or argument. Its implied syllogism is as follows: "All men who habitually lie cannot be trusted. This man habitually lies. Therefore, he cannot be trusted."

[7] Mortimer Adler, "Sense", in *Philosophic Dictionary* (New York: Simon and Schuster, 1995), 178.

Marx, as Charles N.R. McCoy also pointed out, confused the logical and the real orders—a fatal error, as it turns out. The zeal to save "mankind" but do little for individual men is a common error with roots in confusing logic and reality, as is loving "humanity" but not Joseph or Sarah. "At the other extreme from Plato, by an obverse Platonic confusion of the logical and the real," McCoy wrote, "Marx declares the individual man to be the whole of society." [8] Clearly, the individual man cannot be the "whole of society", nor would we want him to be. Society means, as we have seen, an order of many different men doing many different things for a common good that includes the opportunity to do these different things, without which society could not exist.

But we need to understand just why this confusion is possible or even likely. What Marx called the "generic-man" or the "species-man" does not absorb the individual with all his uniqueness into the abstract form of man, as in Plato's forms. Rather, Marx claims to focus this "social" form of all men in the individual so that all are equal because they are all the same, all with the same goods and advantages that came about only because of society. This Marxist endeavor is a mistake of logic. This mistake makes it impossible to see reality in all its form and variety. The "species-man" is an abstraction; it is not John or Sally. What is a reality in the mind is imposed as an ideal criterion on particular reality. The "revolution" consists in making reality conform to the imposed abstraction, thereby destroying all real and lived distinctions in things.

[8] Charles N.R. McCoy, *The Structure of Political Thought* (New York: McGraw-Hill, 1963), 297.

II

Logic is of course related to the Greek word *logos* (λογος), which means reason, or word, or knowledge. It is also the word used for the second Person of the Trinity in the Gospel of John. It refers to the relations within the knowing process we all possess. Logic cannot itself answer a scientific question except questions about itself. But it can provide the tools whereby what is real is correctly analyzed and understood. To do this, however, we must be constantly aware of the difference between mental tools, which are real enough in the mind, and actual beings outside the mind, existing beings to which the mind, as the organ of what we know, looks for its content.

The locus of classical logic is found in six books of Aristotle's *Organon.*[9] These treatises contain the basic analysis of how we identify and name things, how we describe the reality before us, how we attribute one thing of another, how we state what we know and argue to what we do not know, and how we arrive at a knowledge of what a thing is. Logic deals with concepts and propositions, with substances and accidents, with genera and species, with syllogisms, with induction and deduction, and with the four causes. It also deals with sophism, or how to deal with spurious arguments both as to their understanding and as to their persuasiveness. No one really wants to be "illogical". Everyone implicitly assumes that the way he understands things and argues to things follows a valid and defensible process. But it may not so follow. It is the practical task of logic to correct our implicit illogic when it happens.

[9] These books are *The Categories*, *On Interpretation*, *Prior Analytics*, *Posterior Analytics*, *Topics*, and *On Sophistical Refutations*.

It is sometimes argued, moreover, that modern "logic" has made this commonsense approach of Aristotle to be obsolete or irrelevant. Henry Veatch, in his consideration of Aristotle's logic, has examined this question. He has shown that what is known as modern logic, or, better, modern logics, deals with a very different set of relations and presuppositions than those found in Aristotle. These logics, which may be internally consistent with themselves, granted their premises, do not explain or even intend to explain the world which normal people over the ages confronted and in which they have lived.

It was to this latter commonsense experience—Einstein in the capsized boat—to which Aristotle's logic was directed as a way to order. He identified the experience we all share in the actual world. Einstein's rescuers explained to him what he was doing wrong with the sail on a windy day that caused him to capsize. The next day, however, they found him in the same bay, going nowhere in his dinghy. His sail was now tightened against too much wind, as per previous instructions. He had indeed learned one lesson. But since there was no wind that day, Einstein sat still, but uncapsized, in the water. He did not realize that he now needed full sail to move at all. The conflict between common sense and genius is abiding.

"For if the theories of modern science are not based on the facts of experience and really do not reflect them at all," Veatch wrote,

> then perhaps these theories, so far from representing the way things really are in the physical world, reflect instead only the ways in which we have come to view the physical world, the ways we take it to be, and thus the ways in which it is for us. In other words, physical nature appears to the scientist not at all in the way in which it is in itself, but

> only as it is patterned and structured and organized and put together according to the ordering principles which his logic imposes on us. And what might be the consequences of all this then, so far as the status and validity of Aristotle's physics, and indeed of his philosophy as a whole, are concerned? Surely, the consequence would be to leave it all standing pretty much intact.[10]

What Veatch implies, then, is that the world has its own order, originating outside of our minds, but one that is open to our minds and experience. The mind has an order that, when used properly, is itself an instrument to know this world. But it knows after the manner of the knower's mind. The world as we know it, in other words, can be both known and lived in. The simple fact that we know it changes us, but not the world. The acorn does not grow to be a tree in my mind. But I know both what is an acorn and what is an oak and the connection between the two. The tree itself does not know this; it simply is what it is, but it reveals to mind the order of *what it is*.

III

To understand something, we want to see or grasp its order. We see its parts and how they are related to each other and to the purpose of that of which they are parts, to the whole. The first step we take in understanding our own mind, or mind as such, is to notice how things that we know are identified or called. We say, for instance, that Socrates is portly. Socrates is sitting down. Socrates is the father of

[10] Henry Veatch, *Aristotle: A Contemporary Appreciation* (Bloomington: Indiana University Press, 1974), 197.

three boys. But if Socrates is skinny, is running, and has three girls, he is still Socrates, if the latter propositions are in fact true and not the former ones. Both sets of propositions about Socrates, we know from logic, cannot be true at the same time in the same way. We understand, likewise, that these predicates signify different things. To be portly means something other than to be a father. Accidents of quantity, quality, action, relation, and place can change without the substantial being of which they are predicated changing to some other being.

We do not and cannot say, however, that Socrates is Sophocles, or that Socrates is Fido. One substantial being that stands out as a whole in itself cannot be or be said to be another. Each is and remains itself, even if its attributed accidents change. There are distinctions within things that we can and do recognize, as Aristotle tells us, or rather clarifies something we already know. We understand that some things are substances, things that bear reality in themselves, to which we attribute other aspects or predicates. We find that we make these attributions, accidents of substances, all the time.

Hence these knowing operations seem to manifest the nature of our mind in its normal functionings in dealing with what comes before us. We know that we did not give ourselves our own minds or set up the manner of their normal operations. These powers and activities were already operative in us before we ever reflected on them. Still, we can reflectively look back and see what we do when we think and identify things. We can generalize these operations as indicating what things mind does when it acts to know what is not itself. Indeed, only in actively knowing what is not itself can it know itself as now luminous to itself.

Basically, these different attributes that we designate in substances are called accidents, of which there are nine. These nine are quantity, quality, relation, place, time, position, action, passion, and habit. Thus far, we have mentioned quantity (weight), quality (white), action (running), relation (fatherhood), and position (sitting down). Each indicates a different aspect of the reality of something; each is different from and not reducible directly to another. The accidents do not exist by themselves, though they can be understood by themselves. Whiteness does not exist walking down the street, but we can understand it. "Socrates is white" means not that he is "whiteness", but that white is something real in this particular person, though not his essence or substance. Socrates is definitely not green like a frog.

This fact that Socrates is white and not green can lead to "why" questions. "Why is Socrates walking?" Aristotle put the basic issue well:

> Substance, in the truest and primary and most definite sense of the word, is that which is neither predicable of a subject nor present in a subject; for instance, the individual man or horse. But in a secondary sense those things are called substances within which, as species, the primary substances are included; also those which, as genera, include the species. For instance, the individual man is included in the species "man", and the genus in which the species belongs is "animal"; these, therefore—that is to say, the species "man" and the genus "animal"—are termed secondary substances. (2b11–18)

What exists is the individual man, Socrates, or horse, Seabiscuit. Socrates is a man and an animal. Seabiscuit is an animal, not a man. What causes Socrates to be other than

Seabiscuit, that he has reason, is called his difference. The definition of man is hence "the rational animal". This is what he is as distinct from other beings in the universe—gods, animals, plants, rocks.

We can understand whiteness or Fido, what they are, without putting them together. We know what a thing is from what is called "induction". We "induce" from seeing a thing acting in its particular manner. We see a duck. We see another. We see a flock. We see ducklings. We see one this year and another the next. We eat them, see them fly, hear them quack, notice they swim and dive. At some point we arrive at a knowledge of what this particular bird is over against other birds and beings. We know its essence or form. The male mallard has beautiful colors. It is not marked like the male turkey. Our minds are full of things so that we know what they are as distinct from other things.

IV

But knowledge really comes about when we use verbs indicating action. This duck I see is flying. Is that proposition true? It does not depend on the proposition itself but on whether it is in conformity with reality. Does the "is" describe the duck now? Does my mind know what is going on with the duck such that what it affirms, or what I affirm with my mind, is or is not true? "Flying ducks" is something I can understand without affirming that here and now I behold actual ducks actually flying. If the latter is the case, I say, "The duck is flying."

From reflecting on such propositions, we can also learn something about our mind. For example, if it is true that the duck is flying, it is not true that it is not flying. "Duck flying" and "duck not flying" contradict each other, though we can understand both concepts. The principle of contradiction, as we have stated, is the basic intellectual instrument or tool by which we distinguish what we seek to understand from other things, or other things about the same thing. The principle is generally stated as, "A thing cannot be and not be at the same time and in the same circumstances." Nothing, on reflection, is clearer than this affirmation, though we may have to test it to be sure. We cannot exactly prove it. We can, however, show that it cannot be denied without its being simultaneously affirmed.

That is to say, the first or most basic serious intellectual exercise must be to see, by seeking to deny it, why this proposition has to be true. If I affirm that a thing can be and not be at the same time and in the same circumstances, I have tried to deny the truth of the principle. Yet, in denying the principle, I have to affirm logically that this thing, this substance, is also that subject or substance. This tree is this duck—something that could be true if the principle is false. When I recognize that this identity of one thing to another is the implication of my denial of the proposition, I realize consequently that I can affirm nothing of anything. Everything becomes fluid. I have reduced my mind to incoherence so that I know nothing of anything and can know nothing. I cannot deny the principle without denying what it is to be mind, which is the capacity to say this thing is not that thing, the capacity to distinguish.

Moreover, if I say it is not true that the principle of contradiction is true, then my denial must be itself either true or false. There is no third alternative. If my denial-proposition is false—that is, "the principle of contradiction is false"—then the principle remains true. If my proposition is true, then the principle also remains true. In either case, the principle holds, the denial of which destroys the mind as an instrument of any knowledge.

Logic also deals with what are called "deductive syllogisms" and "inductive syllogisms". From the former we want to know whether, from what we know as true, we can conclude to other things as true (or false). From the latter, we want to know how we arrive at the understanding or essence of something such that we can examine what it implies about itself, what things are true of it. It is only when we have understood *what things are* that we can consistently argue to, or conclude to, what other things are.

The syllogism seeks to establish that a proof of something is really a proof, really a valid argument. We want to know both whether what we observe or maintain is true, but also whether the argument by which we explain it to be true is itself valid. Thus, certain things can be true, but the argument presented to show that they are true may be faulty. For instance, take the notion "Socrates is the father of three sons." This is a true proposition, as a matter of fact. Suppose, however, we want to establish this truth by arguing in the following manner: "All Greek males have three sons. Socrates is a Greek male. Therefore, Socrates has three sons." It so happens that the conclusion is true, whatever the argument.

The above argument, as a form of deductive logic, is true: All M is S. P is M. Therefore, P is S. What is wrong? What is wrong is the truth of what is called the "major premise", namely, "All Greek males have three sons." They don't. But the form is correct. It is stated universally. Suppose we argue, "Some Greek males have three sons. Socrates is a Greek male. Therefore, Socrates has three sons." Again the conclusion is true, but there is something wrong with the argument, this time on logical grounds. It is quite true that some Greek males have three sons. And it is true that Socrates is among these. But on the basis of the major premise alone, "Some Greek males have three sons", we cannot necessarily know whether Socrates is one of these, even though he is.

What a syllogism seeks to do is establish a reason why something is true. It gives the basis on which the conclusion is true. Take the commonly used syllogism "All men are mortal. Socrates is a man. Therefore, Socrates is mortal." What is being said here? First of all, the major premise, "All men are mortal", is something whose proof we have first to establish by induction. Once we understand that there is a necessary relation between being a man and dying, we know that this fact of dying is an accident intrinsically connected to what it is to be a man. What about this character, Socrates? What do we know about him just looking at him? Does the mortality business apply to him? Once we are sure he is a man, we can in logic decide, that is, come to know—prove—that he too will die. We may not know from the syllogism that he will die by trial and execution in Athens, about which Plato and Xenephon will write. But we know that he is mortal and so will die.

V

William Wallace, in his book on nature and science, has examined the history of science to ask what were the first real scientific "proofs" that came to be recognized as both logically consistent and as true so that the human mind passed from wondering what was the truth of something to knowing why something is as it is. He indicated that the first scientific proof was that dealing with the cause of the rainbow. What caused the rainbow to look like it did in all its splendor? The assumption was that since rainbows evidently appeared in most places on the planet, always looked more or less the same, and seemed to be related to sun and water, something universal must be happening such that we could definitely determine what a rainbow was.

To understand what a rainbow was, in other words, meant to find its causes—its formal, material, efficient, and final causes. The problem was not whether the rainbow existed—that was obvious—but why it existed. What explained its occurrence such that the mind knew, because of this explanation, what happened? Through a series of experiments and observations of light, rain, and refraction, from Theodore of Freising to Descartes to Newton, the cause of the rainbow came to be more and more certain.[11]

Aristotle had rightly seen that most scientific proofs pass through a gradual process of discovery and perfection. But Aristotle also understood, as Wallace remarks, that the scientist may be reluctant to grant general principles of logical demonstration if they lead to a view that, on other grounds, the scientist may choose to reject. The scientist may have his own theory of the rainbow, associated with his name and fame, that he is reluctant to relinquish.

"Presumably he [Aristotle] was aware that proposing a demonstration to others is not a simple matter", Wallace wrote.

> Those who come upon a truth previously or generally unknown and wish to communicate it to others take on a

[11] William Wallace, *The Modeling of Nature: Philosophy of Science and Philosophy of Nature in Synthesis* (Washington: Catholic University of America Press, 1996), 380–84.

> difficult task. Invariably they must assume the role of teacher, and this brings with it the risk that those to whom they are proposing the demonstration might not wish to be taught. The situation, when transported into the scientific community, by its very nature invites controversy. This is further exacerbated by the content of what is being proposed: a certain and necessary scientific truth, one that cannot be other than it is.[12]

This is a remarkable passage. It points out the very basic difference between the logic of an argument and a human being's willingness to accept that argument if it goes contrary to some prior ideological commitment.

John Lingard, the famous nineteenth-century writer of the *History of England*, put the proper principle well: "My object is truth . . . through the work I made it a rule to tell the truth whether it made for us or not." Yves Simon has, better than almost anyone, shown that acknowledgment of truth for its own sake is central to any order of mind. Simon is author of that principle that can almost stand as the foundation of this book, namely, "Order alone can be the essential cause of order."[13]

It is always difficult to be clearer than Aristotle in teaching us what is order, what is logic, what is reality. "The act of the being of a man", he wrote,

> carries with it the truth of the proposition that he is, and the implication is reciprocal: for if a man is, the proposition wherein we allege that he is is true; and conversely, if the proposition wherein we allege that he is is true, then he is.

[12] Ibid., 377. See the brilliant discussion of truth in Yves Simon, *A General Theory of Authority* (Notre Dame: University of Notre Dame Press, 1980), chapters 3 and 4.

[13] Simon, *General Theory of Authority*, 119.

> The true proposition, however, is in no way the cause of the being of the man, but the fact of the man's being does seem somehow to be the cause of the truth of the proposition, for the truth or falsity of the proposition depends on the fact of the man's being or not being. (14b14–22)

The fact that a man exists is not an issue of logic. The proposition "Man exists", as such, is a matter of logic. Truth happens when we affirm that man is, when in fact he is. Our mind states what reality reveals to us. We distinguish between this thing and that thing. We judge whether this thing exists or does not. We affirm what we know in a proposition that has a definite meaning.

"We suppose ourselves to possess unqualified scientific knowledge of a thing, as opposed to knowing it in the accidental way in which the sophist knows," Aristotle tells us in the *Posterior Analytics*,

> when we think that we know the cause on which the fact depends, as the cause of the fact and of no other, and, further, that the fact could not be other than it is. Now that scientific knowing is something of this sort is evident—witness both those who falsely claim it and those who actually possess it, since the former merely imagine themselves to be, while the latter are also actually, in the condition described. Consequently the proper object of unqualified scientific knowledge is something which cannot be other than it is. (71b8–16)

Aristotle appeals to something that each person can grasp—"something of this sort is evident". If we try to deny it, we again affirm it. "Demonstrative knowledge must rest on necessary basic truths; for the object of scientific knowledge cannot be other than it is" (74b5–6).

I have spent some time with these observations of Aristotle because there are philosophers who want to argue that the human mind does not, as mind, have to accept theoretical propositions as true. It wants to be free of any obligation to the reality that is really what enables it to be mind. The mind is free only when it affirms *what is*. The logic, as Veatch remarked, that Aristotle is concerned with is the logic that explains the mind oriented to stating the truth of things. Truth is precisely the conformity of mind and reality. When presented with the evidence, we are not free to deny arguments that are conclusive, nor should we want to do so.

Yves Simon put the issue well. Our freedom is not a freedom designed to deny the principles of the mind and what it concludes. "In order to express the power of the subject in obvious knowledge," Simon writes,

> many would say that the mind is *forced* or constrained to assent: these words convey pictures of violence which distort the whole situation. When the mind is confronted by an obvious proposition, accompanied by all the conditions of its obviousness, it can neither utter an assent contrary to truth nor withhold its assent and remain silent. The only thing that can be done by act of will is to remove attention. . . . There is no constraint in the necessity that obvious truth brings about in the mind, for constraint is a necessity from without and a violence done to the spontaneity of the subject. When the intellect assents to obvious truth, it acts according to what is most intimate in its own nature. . . . There is nothing more profound in the life of the intellect than our eagerness to know, without tepidity and without fear, under conditions of a certitude totally determined by the power of truth.[14]

[14] Simon, *General Theory of Authority*, 90–91.

The order of mind deals with these things that it seeks to know for their own sakes, to know as true and to know why they are true.

VII

The final topic on the order of mind on which I wish to touch has to do with things that can be otherwise. Here, I want to deal briefly with Aristotle's *Rhetoric*, which concerns persuasion. Human life is full of actions that must be performed either with incomplete knowledge or with a variety of alternatives about what is to be made or done. The mind not only deals with its own structures and its necessary relation to an ordered world of things that cannot be otherwise, but also to things in the world that can be otherwise.

Among the things that can be otherwise are every free human action and the things that are made by man. Such things will be decisions of ethics and politics, of art and craft, of what is to be made or what is to be done. Logic will tell us that if something is already made or decided, it cannot be unmade or undecided. We can seek to do something else on the basis of what was done, but we cannot undo what was done. Again, if Socrates is sitting down, it is eternally true that he did sit down, at this time and place. But it is also true that he did not have to sit down and that he may get up and do something else.

As we noted earlier, Aristotle mentioned the similarity between syllogisms of certainty and those of persuasion. Aristotle was the first systematically to deal with a part of human reality that is constantly before us, namely, the need to decide things with imperfect knowledge or put into effect things that might be done in this way or that, but not in both ways at the same time. If we are going to make a chair, we might have to decide if it will have three legs or four, whether it will have arms, what will be the shape of its back. If we are going to go to the university, we have to decide whether to choose the one in Kansas, the one in Florida, or the one in Chicago. There are good reasons why any of these decisions might be made. Not all our decisions are between good and evil. Some will be between good and good, or even greater or lesser evils.

In any case, we will have to make decisions, and we will seek to influence others who have to make similar decisions. Aristotle talks of differing kinds of situations that will need to be confronted. There are those having to do with a past fact, say, in court. Was this man seen at the crime or not? Evidence points in both directions, but the jury has to be persuaded which was true or more likely.

On the other hand, decisions about the future are based on what avenue of action is more likely to achieve what we want. Will policy A, policy B, or policy C be the best one? Arguments exist for the validity of each alterative, but one must be chosen. Then again, we may want to praise someone, say, in a funeral oration or at a banquet. We seek to convince the audience that this was a good or a bad man, a noble or a knave. We give instances, arguments, and impressions about what the character of the person is. In other words, oratory, or rhetoric, seeks to present us with what arguments work for what sort of cases or situations.

Aristotle had some strong words about the importance of our capacity to persuade people. "It is absurd", he bluntly stated, "to hold that a man ought to be ashamed of being unable to defend himself with his limbs, but not of being unable to defend himself with speech and reason, when the use of rational speech is more distinctive of a human being than the use of his limbs" (1355b1–3). Thus, to be able to defend ourselves or to propose for others arguments and cases that convince people that certain paths should be chosen, that certain judgments should be made, is also a normal and worthy art, the art of persuasion. Many an unjust person has gotten off—and many a just person has been condemned—because of a failure or a success in persuasion. "Rhetoric may be defined as the faculty of observing in any given case the available means of persuasion" (1335b26–27).

Again, I do not intend here to present a short course in rhetoric. But it is necessary to see that this skill is also an aspect of the order of mind as it corresponds to something in normal human reality that is open to understanding and skill. Cicero, the great Roman orator, in his treatise on the subject (*De Inventione*), pointed out that the word "invention", which we tend to think of as related to economics or technology, was actually originally a term from rhetoric, particularly forensic rhetoric. Let us suppose someone was said to have been on the corner of Sixth and Main Street at 7 P.M. on the night a crime was committed. What we need to do is "invent" an explanation that shows that it was impossible for the accused to have been there at that point at that time. By various appeals to logic, passion, and even prejudice, we seek to convince the listeners to see it our way.

Aristotle sums up the matter in this way:

> Rhetorical study, in the strict sense, is concerned with the modes of persuasion. Persuasion is clearly a sort of demonstration, since we are most fully persuaded when we consider a thing to have been demonstrated. . . . The true and

> the approximately true are apprehended by the same faculty; it may also be noted that men have a sufficient natural instinct for what is true, and usually do arrive at the truth. (1355a4–16)

Thus, if we look at this aspect of the mind, it is capable of adjusting itself to the nature of its audience and the moods and passions that are likely to be found there.

Many things have to be decided, and Aristotle is confident that it is worth the effort to use rhetoric even though it does not bring us to that certainty that we find in the theoretical sciences. He finds enough certainty to enable us to create a reasonable order by persuading others what is right. "Rhetoric is useful because things that are true and things that are just have a natural tendency to prevail over their opposites, so that if the decisions of judges are not what they ought to be, the defeat must be due to the speakers themselves, and they must be blamed accordingly" (1355a21–24).

The order of mind, in conclusion, implies not only that the mind has its own peculiar order, as do other spheres of reality, but that the origin of all order, as Socrates noted from Anaxagoras, is somehow mind. The kinds of order that Aquinas noted—that of things, of our free actions, of our makings, and now of our mind—suggest to us that the very life of the mind in its endeavor to know *what is* is a central concern in all philosophy. Just as it is the function of the wise man to order things that are chaotic, so it is the function of mind to recognize other minds and their signs.

When speaking of friendship in his *Ethics*, Aristotle suggested that the subject matter of our highest conversations was precisely the order of things: What is really true? How are things? We do put order into some things, particularly into our polities or our lives or our makings. But we only find the order that is already ourselves and those realities already within us that enable us to know what is not ourselves. In knowing these things, we come to know also something of ourselves.

Logic does not deal with the existence and nature of external objects. Even the genius has to deal with a capsized boat in a practical way so that it sails on Peoconic Bay rather than capsizes. We are not abstractions subsumed into forms, nor are we the whole of reality identified with ourselves. As Simon said, "There is nothing more profound in the life of the intellect than the desire to know." At some point we need to ask ourselves both what it is to know and what is there to know. Our minds are capable of knowing *all that is*, though we must proceed in an orderly fashion and we know only step by step. Aristotle tells us not to listen to those who tell us to occupy ourselves only with things that can be otherwise. But he did not mean that we are to neglect knowing the things that can be otherwise and what it is that our mind does when it knows them.

CHAPTER VII

THE ORDER OF HELL

After they have been carried along to the Acherusian lake, they cry out and shout, some for those they have killed, others for those they have maltreated, and calling them they then pray to them and beg them to allow them to step out into the lake and to receive them. If they persuade them, they do step out and their punishment comes to an end; if they do not, they are taken back into Tartarus and from there into the rivers, and this does not stop until they have persuaded them they have wronged, for this is the punishment which the judges imposed on them.

—Plato *Phaedo* 114a–b

And those who do good, they will go to eternal life; to those who do evil, however, to eternal fire. This is the Catholic faith, which, unless someone firmly and faithfully believes it, he cannot be saved.

—Athanasian Creed, A.D. 400[1]

Between us and heaven or hell there is only life, which is the frailest thing in the world.

—Pascal *Pensées* 213

[1] *Et qui bona egerunt, ibunt in vitam aeternam, qui vero mala, in ignem aeternum. . . . Haec est fides catholica, quam nisi quisque fideliter firmiterque crediderit, salvus esse non poterit.*

I

Hell, in its philosophic dimensions, is not first or primarily a revelational doctrine, though it is found in revelation also. In the New Testament, we find a famous passage in which Christ remarks of Beelzebub, the Devil, that if he does not have an "order" within his own kingdom, how can he stand? This is a curious statement. Plato had implied a similar idea in the first book of the *Republic*, in which he pointed out that unjust men are stronger and more dangerous if they manage to agree on their own internal organization or order in carrying out their crimes against others. Just as a common good is stronger when all the parts work and belong together in accomplishing what is worthy, so an organization or polity is more dangerous if it is well organized in working against what is good. We are tempted to think that simple disorder or chaos is the worst evil, but these passages suggest that the worst evil itself has some organization, some order that can be spelled out.

Aristotle, in his treatment of the worst tyrant in the *Politics*, brought up another aspect of this same question. In seeking the intelligible essence of what a true tyrant is, Aristotle argued that the tyrant ran the worst regime. What did this mean? The background of this question was also in the first book of the *Republic*, wherein it was proposed that the tyrant, because he could get whatever he wanted, was the happiest of men. It was, for the sake of argument, the supposition of the *Republic* of Plato to show that the tyrant was in fact the unhappiest of men because he looked only to himself. Everything was ordered to his own private good, such that the tyrant could be sure that nothing was given to him or done for him out of any pure or unselfish motives.

What is important here to realize is the kind of order that is found in the most disordered regime, the tyranny. It parallels the disorder within the individual soul. Aristotle classified all bad regimes as bad because their ruling principle, whether it be one, few, or many, ruled not for the common good but for itself, for the good of the ruling principle. In the case of the tyrant, he ruled for his own private good as if it were also the common good to which all else was subjected. But he was more dangerous than the disordered man without political power because not only was the tyrant's own inner soul ordered to a good that excluded others, but other institutions and people within the polity were also ordered to this personal private good. In other words, the tyrant was someone who had managed, through fear or power or even affection, to order everything to his own good. He was never able to get outside of himself. The tyrant becomes a paradigm of an intelligible order of disorder.

The ancient writers never considered the tyrant to be untalented or unattractive. Quite the opposite. He possessed all the talents of the philosopher and all the charm of a man of the world. He was not physically repulsive. His disorder was not a lack of basic knowledge but a reordering of all that fell under his control not to their proper ends but to himself as their proper end. We sometimes speak of modern "totalitarian" states as worse than classical (or contemporary) tyrannies. Generally, we do this because of the awesome psychological and physical power of the modern state. In particular we are concerned with the claim of the totalitarian state also to control our minds and beliefs in the name of the good of the ideology or state.

Aristotle would not have been overly surprised at this consequence. He had already laid down several principles that have become the essence of ordered tyrannies. The first is that no one be allowed to have friends. All relationships are to be public and known by the authorities. Secondly, all are to be kept busy and fairly exhausted so that little energy is left over for political mischief. By these means, each citizen is kept isolated from the others and unable to act.

The problem of hell first arose in such a political context. Hell as a doctrine or question did not arise because some absent god imposed it on mankind. Rather, it arose out of the oft-observed political fact that tyrants are not punished for their crimes. They are often successful and die with honors in their beds in spite of all of their crimes and injustices. To be sure, some tyrants are punished in this world. But the doctrine of hell is related to the obviously grave and unpunished crimes that occur within the world.

The polity itself was originally formed, in part, to punish violations of justice. The doctrine of hell arose over the question of whether, ultimately, the world was just. If crimes were not punished and virtues rewarded, then it seemed that all was disordered and in vain. Hell, a judgment and punishment beyond the political order, arose as a logical solution to this problem. Ultimately, all crimes were punished, all virtues rewarded. The world was not ill made. The relation of creation to the inner life of the Godhead, as a result, was not contradictory.

II

The doctrine of hell often scandalizes the modern world, and not a few in the contemporary Church. It is embarrassing, it is said, to be saddled with this "outmoded" and supposedly unnecessary notion. Yet it is modernity's most neglected doctrine. I have often wondered why. After all, as I have mentioned, it is an ancient teaching found in Plato, found in Scripture, found in many religious and philosophic sources. It has its own iron logic, the denial of which leads to very unpleasant consequences for human worth. These consequences, in fact, are themselves revelatory of the "order" that hell portrays. Pascal tells us that between heaven or hell stands "only life", the "frailest" of things. Evidently, Pascal thought that after even our frailness is destroyed—that is, our finite lives—our sole alternative is either heaven or hell. In other words, these finite lives have transcendent significance, or they would simply disappear into nothingness.

This passage in Pascal echoes that found in the Gospel of Matthew, wherein, in the final Judgment, all are pictured as being inevitably separated into those who are saved and those who are lost. "Next he will say to those on his left hand, 'go away from me, with your curse upon you, to the eternal fire prepared for the devil and his angels'" (Mt 25:41–42). Augustine made this same distinction between the City of God and the City of Man, to neither of which city can anyone belong involuntarily. This voluntary belonging to either city is again the reason why the primary point of relationship between the inner life of God and what is not God is the intelligence and will of a being that is not God but who can will to receive what the Godhead is about in its internal life.

John Adams, the second American President, held that hell is the Christian doctrine most necessary to politics. For without it, the state would conceive, as its own mission, the duty of punishing all vices, secret and public. But to do that would require a divine mind and a totalitarian state apparatus. Therefore, Adams implied, politics is limited, as Saint Thomas also said, to the external forum, to dealing with the most public and dangerous crimes. In any state, many crimes will go unpunished. We have to accept this limitation at the risk of greater evils. This is why, even as we see in Plato, the doctrine of hell has also a political origin, for the human mind cannot accept the idea that ultimately terrible and numerous crimes will go unpunished, even if the state cannot be the total instrument of their punishment.

Following Plato's theological imagery in the *Phaedo*, however, we like to think that, no matter what we do, there is always a second or third or one hundredth chance to amend our ways and repair the damage we cause. No decision about hell, we like to think, can really be "final", hence the desperate, though not totally heretical, wish that, even if it exists, no one is in it. Sooner or later, we like to think, someone will come to our rescue to declare that what we did was not wrong after all. Or that we need not acknowledge its heinousness. Or again, we insist that someone will forgive us, either in this world or the next, without our having to do anything, without our having actively to participate in the process.

Some reincarnation theories, besides being intimations of a desire of resurrection of the body, as opposed to theories of immortality of the soul, are designed so that we do not have to face squarely the doctrine of the eternity of hell. They postulate an unending series of reincarnations, even into animals, an unending series of new choices until we finally get it right, presumably somewhere down the ages. Thus, eventually, no one is lost, which seems to be the ultimate purpose of all reincarnation theories. That is, they are designed to reject the doctrine of hell, of final decision against the good.

This thesis apparently saves God from the presumably unwanted necessity of carrying out His own stern rules and order. A God who cannot or will not by His wisdom or power save everyone, no matter what they think or do, is said to be an inferior, a less-than-all-powerful, totally insensitive God. Yet such theories, when spelled out, deny us the reality and finality of our choices and hence the drama on which our dignity is based. They propose a semi-eternity of choosing not to choose our final fate, in which we rest in either a paradise or a hell. Still, it is the purpose of human life to make this very choice. The purpose of creation is precisely that a free choice of the highest things be made in order that the highest things may in fact exist in our souls.

Salvation or redemption does not depend only or wholly on ourselves, of course. Any honest self-reflection reveals that we are finite, limited beings. We did not give ourselves either being or life, nor did we give ourselves what-it-is-to-be-ourselves, the kinds of beings we find ourselves to be. We are, at bottom, receivers, even of ourselves. This is what the fact that the world need not exist means. What causes us to be human beings and not turtles—if you will, our natures—are likewise not products of our own willing. This does not deny the fact that we can will to reject even what we are. We can reject our own very order of existence.

Divine omnipotence, it is sometimes maintained, can always change its mind about our troubled record, or even about its own eternal intentions. In pure voluntarist theories of the Godhead, God is held to be pure will. Thus, He is said not to be limited by His own rules or even by the principle of contradiction, the first law of being. God is absolute freedom, limited by nothing, even by the distinction of right and wrong. By an act of His will, it is claimed in this system, He can even make right to be wrong and wrong to be right. Even the famous French philosopher Jacques Maritain speculated that maybe God could or would reduce Lucifer's eternal punishment. But if Lucifer's final status could be changed, how much more human conditions and choices? Eternity, on this hypothesis, turns out to be rather more changeable than we have at first been led to believe.

These are what I call "sympathetic theories" about hell. They look on hell from the hypothetical viewpoint of the one said to be simmering there because of God's rigid judgment about something He could change with a mere flip of the will. The contemplation of pain often dulls the sense of justice. Suffering, even just suffering as punishment for terrible deeds, causes compassion. A God "inventing" or "willing" a hell appears to be a harsh God. We say something like, "If I were God, I would not make anyone to suffer, no matter what he did." The implied conclusion to this line of reasoning is thus: "If I would not do something, neither would God." God ends up looking remarkably like ourselves, that is, rather arbitrary and wishy-washy. We do not conform to God's world, but He to ours.

If, then, we insist on looking at hell from the point of view of the condemned *qua* sufferers and not *qua* guilty, I suspect we will never understand the depths and order of this most interesting and perplexing of doctrines. Nor will we see the logic behind it—and there is a logic behind it. It is to that ordered logic that we address ourselves here. If we smugly declare our superiority to God by claiming that we would not do what He did, we can suspect that we did not really understand the implications of the divine purposes for the world in the first place. The doctrine of hell has a place in the order of things that, by its very existence, upholds what is noblest and most desirable in our being, the integral freedom we have to choose what is true and good not because we are commanded to do so but because we see that this is what reality is about.

III

Plato had it right, of course, in the passage cited at the beginning of this chapter. Our sins could be forgiven, though only if we acknowledged them. But also, in Plato, the victim who suffered from them specifically had to forgive us. We could not simply forgive ourselves. Our deeds still mattered, and mattered to others. Plato implicitly emphasized this latter point in his picturing the damned, from the river, pleading for forgiveness from those whom they injured or killed. Thus, he seems to have understood that salvation does not primarily depend on us, even when it also does depend on us, on our pleading for forgiveness. Not only is sinning a relation to others, so is its forgiveness. Indeed, if our actions have a transcendent effect, they will have to call upon this source also. Evidently, God takes us more seriously than we normally are wont to admit.

The Christian gloss on this Platonic position is that sin not only harms ourselves and usually someone else, but it "harms" God in harming one of His creatures. There is here a hint of trinitarian order even in disorder. Sin is not just between me and the one I offend. Thus, forgiveness takes on a divine dimension. God, in loving us, can, as it were, "feel" the harm that others do to us or we to them.

This is part of the dynamic of love that ends eventually in the Crucifixion of the God-man, in what is called the Atonement. Ultimately, by ourselves, we cannot escape our own sins. For this escape, we depend on the love and sacrifice of another. We must, in other words, acknowledge our own inability to stop all the evils we let loose in the world. Sin has a contagion to it in its influence on the wills of others, though out of it can come both good and evil. Because I sin, it does not follow that you *must* sin; because you do good, it does not follow that I cannot do evil in return. Such is our freedom.

Plato's notion of punishment, moreover, is connected with the question of forgiveness. He maintained that we should want to be punished for our sins and crimes precisely to restore the order we violated in committing them. By our desire to be punished for what we actually did, we acknowledge an order whose validity we now uphold by our repentance. Plato explained the extremes of vindictiveness in the *Gorgias*. There he held that the worst punishment we could inflict on someone with a serious crime on his soul was *not* to punish him. We cannot help but recognize the genius of this view. If we did not punish someone, he would remain in his crime. We would let him be destroyed. Thus, without repentance, he would remain eternally unrepentant. He would be stuck in his soul's permanent disorder and punishment, condemned to a place called Tartarus, or Hades, or hell.

Hell is never to repent, never to choose what is not ourselves. This theme was also found in *Hamlet*, the waiting to kill a man precisely when he was in the act of serious sin, deliberately giving him no time for repentance. To follow and pursue this vindictive course against someone was itself, no doubt, a grave sin. Killing a man so he could not repent was the extreme of the refusal to love our enemy, an enemy who in his very deed was engaged in an act offensive to God. In this sense, the eternity or even the punishment of hell has nothing to do with hell, but with the will of the person who decides to go there by his refusal to acknowledge that what is right is, after all, right.

In Scripture, the principal occupant of hell, as we have intimated, seems to be a fallen angel by the name, among others, of Satan or Lucifer. We should not miss the symbolism of his name, Lucifer, the "light bearer". He was among the most intelligent of the angels. He remains an angel even in hell. He is not demoted to human or animal status. This is why he remains so dangerous. This fact alone should alert us to reflect that the connection between spirit and evil may be much closer than the connection of body and evil, as we are more likely to think. The whole history of the heresy known as Gnosticism, the idea of self-salvation by our own knowledge, with its Manichean codicil that marriage is evil, is a proof of this point.

Satan, moreover, has tended to steal every show or play in which he appears, most famously in Milton's *Paradise Lost.* Why is this? we might wonder. Ever since Sisyphus, there has been a kind of romance in the defiance of the gods, something easily projected onto Lucifer himself. "True humanism", or "atheistic humanism", is said to be found in the "rebel" who, in the name of his own unlimited freedom, rejects the natural law of what it is to be a human being.

Christ once suggested that the Devil's kingdom is not divided against itself. While that diabolic unity does not necessarily make satanic organizations ideal places in which to work, it does make them uncommonly dangerous. At a minimum, this diabolical harmony means that such a kingdom is stronger in pursuing its dire purposes than it would be by individual disorder, a point, as we have seen, also made by Plato in book I of the *Republic* when talking about the tyrant.

The children of darkness are often more enterprising than the children of light. Our struggle is not against flesh and blood, but against principalities and powers. And what is the purpose of this kingdom "not divided against itself"? Evidently, its principal endeavor is to entice, cajole, or persuade rational creatures freely to cast themselves into that "eternal fire" of which the Athanasian Creed spoke, following Matthew. No doubt the most bemused account of this process is found in C. S. Lewis' *The Screwtape Letters*.

Generally speaking, it has been my experience that, when many are pretty much agreed that this or that Christian doctrine is untenable or wrong, then it is the precise time when such a denied doctrine is most relevant and, more than that, most intelligible and most needed. It is my view that the best case to be made for the reality of hell is to examine the views that maintain that it does not and cannot exist. Even though the universe is full of flaming infernos of various types, no spacecraft has reported sighting precisely hell. We are probably, even on theological grounds, not too surprised by the failure of spacecraft to spot the "eternal flames". For, at the present moment, hell could be occupied only by fallen angels or human damned souls, neither of which are corporeal.

This information may not be particularly consoling, however, since there is such a thing as spiritual suffering, what is called sometimes "the pain of loss", the knowing that we are missing that for which we exist. Likewise, Scripture tells of the resurrection of the body, telling us that this resurrection will also include the bodies of the damned, whoever they might be. The logical alternative is either that everyone is resurrected, whether he be saved or damned, or no one is. The denial of the resurrection of the body is often an attempt to cut off at the pass any worry about actual and eternal punishment for the particular kind of beings we are—persons composed of bodies and souls. But Plato had already prevented this avenue by proving precisely that the immortality of the soul was designed not to destroy the soul but to keep it so that, if need be, it could be punished or rewarded.

But someone might say, "Come now, level with us; surely this doctrine of hell is a gigantic myth, a hoax, an analogy, a scare tactic." I am going to approach this issue from perhaps a different angle. Catholicism is an intellectual religion. If it holds something to be true, it has reasons for this claim, reasons that should be valid in logic and in evidence. Faith is directed to reason and does not contradict it. Indeed, it improves it. This intellectual consistency means that a doctrine of revelation will find at least indirect confirmation in reason and will. When wrestling to figure out what a given doctrine means, the very effort will generally cause reason to become more itself, more reason. In this sense, the doctrine of hell is one that incites the intellect as does no other. All of the efforts to deny or mitigate this doctrine do not result in the intellectual stimulus that the orthodox doctrine provides.

I am going to suggest that if we think correctly about hell, it will not seem like such an outlandish teaching as it is often pictured to be. Someone may still want to reject it. I have no problem with that provided I can examine the grounds of the rejection. But I think, on analysis, that the basis for the rejection will usually be more in the order of sentiment or compassion than hard thought. Moreover, I will suggest, paradoxically, that the doctrine of hell has something rather consoling, even ennobling, about it. We are not really prepared for what we must logically give up if this doctrine is not true. Reflection on this teaching, furthermore, will assist in putting together a number of other things for which we sometimes see no purpose.

IV

Let me begin by observing that the doctrine of hell is both a philosophic position and a teaching of revelation. This double source itself has some significance, namely, why do both sources agree? Do they both have a common origin? The doctrine of hell, in its complete understanding, requires that we maintain that the world, including the human world, has an order. It is not a chaos, the opposite of order. Indeed, we affirm with Genesis that the world and all in it are created to be good. Neither material nor human things are, as such, evil, though there are philosophies that maintain otherwise. Within that order, an effort must be made to account for reality as it actually is. The doctrine of hell, on reflection, is not absurd or unintelligible.

To see this fact more clearly, I will cite an observation made by the Anglican philosopher Eric Mascall:

> The doctrine of the absurdity of existence is the natural climax of the process of secularization which has increasingly characterised the thought and activity of the modern world. That is to say, if you try to find the ultimate meaning of the world simply within it you will fail, and then, if you refuse to look for it anywhere else, you will say that the world does not make sense. If you develop a neurosis as a result, this will be the effect of your conclusion rather than its cause.[2]

[2] E. L. Mascall, *The Christian Universe* (the Boyle Lectures, 1965) (Darton, Longman & Todd, 1966), 34–35.

Existence is not absurd. The doctrine of hell, furthermore, is not an argument that would imply that it is—just the opposite, in fact.

But if we try to find the ultimate meaning of the world wholly within it, we will indeed fail. If we refuse to look to the whole body of information available to us, probably the world will not make sense. If we become neurotic because we cannot deal with hell, the cause is probably due to our own choices rather than some proper account of the order of things. An absurd world causes neurosis to a mind that sees only this absurdity. The doctrine of hell is not absurd. It stands at the other side of free will, even though there are those who deny free will precisely so that they cannot be held responsible for their actions. But if free will is indeed absurd, then it really does not make any difference whether we believe in hell or not, for in a determined world, we can believe only what we must, even if we believe in hell.

Let me state too that when we maintain that we can understand any Christian dogma, including hell, we do not mean that we can totally or completely fathom its depths. We do not claim for ourselves the depths of the divine mind. But this does not mean that we know nothing, nor does it mean that what we do know is not true. Christianity does not relate to what it does state and formulate as if its defined understanding totally exhausts the subject matter. On the other hand, just because, with the power of the human mind alone, Christianity does not fathom the depths of reality, it does not follow that what it does know is therefore false. Christianity retains the Socratic wisdom that says that its wisdom is to know what it does not know. George MacDonald, the Scottish theologian, put it well: "The darkness knows neither the light nor itself; only the light knows itself and the darkness also. None but God hates evil and understands it."[3] We might likewise state that no one but God knows hell and understands it.

MacDonald will also give us our first formal statement about hell: "The one principle of hell is—'I am my own.'"[4] This statement is important because it shifts our attention away from the "eternal fires" or sufferings said to be in hell to the more central issue of the reasons why anyone might be in hell. These reasons have something to do with the order of things. We have perhaps heard Sartre's famous quip that "hell is the other", a view directly opposite to that life pictured in the Trinity, where even God is other. The position of Sartre, like MacDonald's statement, implies that the self is sufficient, that nothing but the self can enter into our calculations, that we certainly should have no dependency on anything but ourselves. Note too that this definition of hell is the direct opposite of the classical definition of love—to will the good of another for the sake of the other.

Since there is no error that does not contain some truth, we can see that what lies behind the statements of MacDonald and Sartre is the affirmation of the centrality and existence of a self or a person. What is rejected is anything that makes demands on the self, any rules or laws that the self did not make. This is a world of what appears to be infinite loneliness, of the view that others are threats or mere tools to be used for ourselves. There is no room for any love or generosity or gift that would imply a good or delight in anything other than the self. It is a formula for isolation, again exactly the opposite of the inner life of the Godhead. Indeed, one of the classic definitions of hell is

[3] *George MacDonald: An Anthology*, ed. C. S. Lewis (New York: Macmillan, 1947), no. 364, p. 148.

[4] MacDonald, *Anthology*, no. 203, p. 88.

that it is the choice to be oneself forever, almost as if one were a self-made god. This is generally how the vice of pride has been described in Greek and Christian literature. We touched on this point in regard to the tyrant. The self has no relation to another except in terms of itself. The legitimate endeavor to recognize that the human being is something of great worth ends up with the affirmation that it is the only worth.

Perhaps we can gain further light from the structure of Plato's *Republic*, which ends, significantly, with a consideration of hell that arises out of precisely the failure of any existing polity to establish true justice. One of the main driving forces behind Plato's *Republic* was the realization that the virtue of justice, in its highest form, could not be found in any existing human polity. Cities were established to render each his due, to render justice. The need for justice meant that injustice existed on a widespread scale.

But even when the civic regimes were established, as we have seen, injustices remained in spite of the judicial and penal systems, something that would surprise no one familiar with the doctrine of original sin. What Plato realized is that the human mind cannot remain content with the notion that injustices are not eventually punished. For if injustice is not punished and if virtue is not rewarded in these same cities, it must mean either they are requited someplace else or that the universe, from a moral standpoint, is "in vain", to use Aristotle's term. In other words, there is really no order in the highest things.

The *Republic* of Plato thus postulated the existence of rewards and punishments for what actually took place in the world to lie outside of the world, in the hands of God. It is quite clear that, in any historically existing polity, all the vices are not punished, even when some are, nor are all the virtuous deeds rewarded, even if some are. Indeed, in existing polities, often vices are rewarded handsomely while virtues are suppressed. When contemplating this perplexing situation, the human mind is deeply restless. It is tempted to think that there is something enormously wrong with the world. As Adeimantus said in the second book of the *Republic*, the poets picture the tyrants to be happy while the good appear to be punished, just the opposite order from what it should be. Surely, if this be true, something is terribly wrong with the world.

The answer to this situation is that the human soul is immortal. Nothing can destroy it, as Plato takes pains to show in the *Phaedo* and in the *Republic*. The logic behind this position is that we bear our crimes with us so that we are judged not according to our own self-made standards or our city's standards, but by the standards of justice itself. Hell, in this sense, is the result of the incomprehensible idea that injustice is ultimately not punished. In other words, when we get rid of the reality of hell, we implicitly agree that injustice succeeds. That is, we accept the idea that the order of the world itself is not well made, that it does not originate in the good.

V

Yet another way to approach the notion that there might be something to be said for hell is from the practical consequences of its denial. For the sake of argument, let us grant that there is no hell, no ultimate consequences of our ill deeds. Whether we are virtuous or vicious, we all end up in the same place. Presumably we are all saved, even without formal repentance. Repentance is designed to limit the consequences of our evil actions by ourselves acknowledging that they are indeed evil. As I hinted earlier, there is something romantic about even hell. It makes our lives dramatic, full of consequences. It makes an ultimate difference what we do or do not do.

To be sure, this is a paradox. But let me see if I can explain what I mean. Human lives are full of daily deeds of many sorts—some usual, some unusual; some clearly noble, some clearly vicious. This situation carries on throughout our lives, however long we live. If we are sure that there are no ultimate consequences to any act of ours, no matter what we do, we are left with a certain liberty to do evil with impunity, whatever theory we might use to explain it. If each human life is, in fact, a drama, as I like to think that it is, this drama has meaning only if what we do makes a difference. If it makes no real difference whether we be virtuous or vicious, in whatever category we choose to discuss, then our encounters with others are really of no importance. Perhaps this is what MacDonald and Sartre were getting at.

But if the doctrine of hell is true, if it is a real possibility for each person as a result of his actual choices, of his putting disorder into his soul and into the world, it means that our ordinary affairs are shot through with unimaginable significance. At any time of any day of our lives, we can do something of ultimate reward or damnation. Our deeds are not mere blips on the screen of eternity. They are acts that demand judgment, demand order. Human lives are of ultimate importance, not because they made themselves so, but because of what they are, something that they did not themselves establish by their own choices or powers. To be sure, modern voluntarism from Nietzsche and rationalism from Descartes and Kant postulate an absolute independence or autonomy of the self. But whatever the human being is, it is not something of its own creation, though its final personal destiny is indeed something of its own choice.

What the doctrine of hell does, then, is guarantee that our lives are not merely things of a moment. Rather, they are things full of instances. At each instance, we could choose salvation or damnation. This is because what we are is rooted in a love that we did not give ourselves. I mentioned earlier that we could, in a way, "wound" God, just as we can wound our parents or spouses or friends by doing an act that harms someone we love.

Looked at from this point of view, I think, the doctrine of hell stands at the basis of romanticism—that is, our loves do make a difference. Love is not just any old emotion or pleasure, but it is choosing and willing the good of another, for that person's own sake. This means that our lives, our pedestrian lives, are charged with significance. It also means that whether we are rich or poor, great or small, we are all players in the same drama involving those among whom our human lives are lived.

Thus, hell, on examination, is not such an outlandish teaching as we might at first think. It falls into a higher order. It undergirds the very significance of our daily actions. It reinforces our sense that the world contains an intelligible order. The only way to eliminate the doctrine of hell would be, I think, to eliminate the doctrine of the freedom of the will, the possibility of finite persons with relations to what is not themselves. But if we eliminate that doctrine, we cease to be finite, rational beings responsible for our own destiny and our own understanding of the worth of others.

Hell, moreover, does not exist apart from a doctrine of forgiveness. This has something to do with Saint Thomas' position that the world was created in mercy, not in justice. That is, the Platonic worry that justice is not requited is modified by the Platonic and Christian notion of forgiveness. But the one thing that God cannot do is create a free being and not allow him to be free. This is why hell has long been associated with the notion of self-enclosure. Hell is an eternity of ourselves. Hardly any punishment seems more severe than this, than the rejecting of all else but ourselves. The only thing we encounter in such a world is, alas, ourselves, but we know that we did not make ourselves to exist or to be what kind of being we are. Lucifer also knew this of himself. Hell is not the other. Hell is ourselves with the realization that this narrow "good" is what we chose and with the added realization that we alone have refused to be open to any alternative.

Thus, to return to the central theme of this book, hell is not a proof that the world lacks order, but a proof that it betrays it even in the most fundamental of things. We can reasonably maintain that the internal order of hell is the way that we seek to make everything, including other persons—including God—revolve around ourselves. The self around which we seek to order things, however, is itself not of our making. It too is related to what is other. It retains its intrinsic personal orientation to that other that explains the kind of being that it is, that it does not make but discovers itself to be. Hell is not an argument against order, but an argument for the overall order in which all things, including aberrant and evil things, have their intelligible place.

CHAPTER VIII

THE ORDER OF REDEMPTION

Then, let's begin our dialogue by reminding ourselves of the point at which we began to discuss the nature that someone must have if he is to become a fine and good person. First of all, if you remember, he had to be guided by the truth and always pursue it in every way, or else he'd really be a boaster, with no share at all in true philosophy.

—Plato *Republic* 489e–90a

What is the source of man's greatness? Scripture says: *The man who boasts must boast of this, that he knows and understands that I am the Lord.* Here is man's greatness, here is man's glory and majesty: to know in truth what is great, to hold fast to it, and to seek glory from the Lord of glory. . . . Boasting of God is perfect and complete when we acknowledge that we are utterly lacking in true righteousness and have been made righteous only by faith in Christ.

—Basil the Great, Homily, *De humilitate*[1]

Long ago, even before he made the world, God chose us to be his very own, through what Christ would do for us; he decided then to make us holy in his eyes, without a single fault—we who stand before him covered with his love.

—Ephesians 1:4 (*Living Bible*)

[1] Basil the Great, Homily 20, *De humilitate* 3, in *The Liturgy of the Hours*, Monday, Office of Readings, Third Week of Lent.

I

The admonition of Plato that we must be guided by the truth and pursue it in every way is something that is also essential in Christianity's understanding of itself and, indeed, of what is not itself. We are, as Basil the Great said, "to know in truth what is great". We do not give ourselves righteousness, or even less, make it to be what it is. It is something we receive and become. We know that we do not constitute by ourselves *what it is*. Though we know things by our natural reason, we are righteous only by faith in Christ. In a sense, the modern world is a place where every definition of salvation—this-worldly or spiritual—except this one is accepted.

Even at our "beginning", however, we are already in a sense begun—"even before the beginning of the world, God chose us", as Saint Paul said. We are "covered" by a love in all that we do. This is a remarkable statement since it is that "cover" alone that can overcome our faults and sins, of which there are many. We are not to be made holy by our own powers, but we are to be holy nonetheless. The order of redemption is about being made holy, about its way that is not our way. Being holy means that our sins are also forgotten, forgiven—not denied, but acknowledged. Yet this forgiveness has a price that we did not ourselves first pay. Salvation is also about understanding how it is possible that we sin and how it is not possible that we redeem ourselves. It is about how it is possible that we are redeemable and subsequently about how this redemption was carried out and can continue to be carried out.

An order of creation is thinkable without an order of redemption, but an order of redemption is not thinkable without an order of creation. An order of redemption implies that something went wrong within the order of creation, though not necessarily because of or outside of the ken of the origin of creation in the first place. The realization that something could go radically wrong in a free creature is why we also, in the previous chapter, treated of order in hell. But redemption also implies a noncontradictory way to restore or to attempt to restore that disrupted order, or even to improve it. Because of the very nature of freedom, of free will, an order of redemption will probably succeed only for the most part, even if that. In any case, it is worth the effort to seek to restore order once it is broken. The very effort will reveal something about the Godhead that we never could otherwise have expected, as Aquinas said in dealing with God's mercy.

The order of hell is simply the ultimate and dire consequence of what could have gone wrong in the order of creation and, in fact, did go wrong. But not everyone who "went wrong" at some point ends up in hell, as seems to have been the case with those angels who refused any elevation offered to their freedom. While the ultimate status of angels and men can be the same in principle, their situation is different in their power and perception.

The order of redemption is about the way in which what did go wrong among human beings was, if possible, to be repaired and by whom. Not just any scheme of redemption would have been adequate but only one in which the Redeemer is Himself of the Godhead—the Son of God, in fact. Nor would He have been adequate were He not also true man—one person, two natures. Redemption, in other words, is the way that the original plan of God, the original order, is achieved so that God's purpose in creation in the first place, to associate other free beings in his inner trinitarian life, is achieved within an order of actual being that includes the Fall.

II

We have seen the principle of Saint Thomas that grace builds on nature. But it is not the primary purpose of redemption, of grace, simply to assist the natural world to be natural, to be what it is already intended to be. It can have this effect indirectly, but this is not its primary purpose. Redemption implies restoration, but it also implies the elevation already implicit in creation's initial purpose. If Aristotle argued that happiness was that end for which we acted in all that we did, redemption addresses itself to a fuller understanding of what this happiness entails for the actual human beings who exist in this order of creation. It results in a more complete spelling out, as it were, of the implications of happiness in the sort of rational creature that we are.

Saint Thomas, as we have seen, often cites the famous phrase "*sapientis est ordinare*"—the function of the wise man is to order, to put things in order. We human beings have the added burden, if I can call it that—for it is also a glory—of cooperating in the ordering of ourselves and of all those things that are open to our knowing and making. We have called it the order of soul (chapter 4). To order also means that we properly place ourselves amid the other things, including human things, that are not ourselves. We see the relation of things to each other. When things are not working properly, we put up signs indicating that the devices are "out of order". The repairman is someone who restores order to what is not functioning because some aspect of the whole, some part, is not doing what it should be doing or else the whole is not going where it should be going.

We human beings have a certain nobility. We stand outside of nothingness as persons, as those who know and know that they know. Psalm 8 says that we are "a little less than the angels". We are not gods. We are not angels. But we are what we are. We can even protest what we are. We can think that it is unjust that we are what we are or that we are in the existential situation that we are. We can even deny that we are well made.

Aristotle remarked that man, when he is good, is the best of the animals, but when he is bad, he is the worst. Our defiance of what we are is not merely a statement of fact. It bears the mark of a chosen, positive opposition, as if we are talking to someone, protesting something that we think ought to be otherwise or perhaps not be at all. C. S. Lewis, in a famous passage in *Mere Christianity*, noticed that if we listen carefully to ordinary people engaged in controversy or altercation, everyone will insist on giving reasons for what he does, especially when what he does is considered to be wrong.[2] No one does what is wrong without at least claiming a reason that explains why what he did is right.

But we protest too much. We want God or someone else to make us free, almost as if we do not want the burden of being actually free. If this unchosen aid is not forthcoming, if we are not simply given all that we want on our own terms, we claim the power to make our own freedom, freed, so we think, of obligation to that which made us. But God has said that the only way we can be free is to know the truth, the truth of things, the truth of what we are. And we can, and frequently do, choose not to know the truth. How seldom do we reflect on this enormous power we have to reject the truth, to claim that *what is* is not. But this capacity is the negative side of the equally tremendous

[2] C. S. Lewis, *Mere Christianity* (New York: Macmillan, [1943] 1975), chap. 1.

power that we have to affirm that there is a truth and that we can recognize it and delight in it.

I like to think that God, when He created us, took what I call "the risk of God". That is, He could have chosen, with no contradiction in Himself, *not* to create us, so that nothing would have possibly gone wrong.[3] In a way of speaking, in retrospect, not creating anything would have saved Him a considerable amount of trouble. Because of the fullness of His inner life (chapter 2), God was not necessitated to create, or to create precisely us or this kind of world in which the Incarnation and Redemption are found at its present heart. We underestimate the Godhead if we suppose that God, if He knew us from the "beginning", did not know what human choice entailed, both for glory and for damnation. It certainly entailed the fact that we could and would, at some level, choose to reject God. For so doing, we would claim "virtue" or "freedom" or "independence" or "autonomy" for ourselves.

Did the fact that man did choose himself over God suggest an imperfection in God? Or did it, rather, indicate a perfection in Him as well as in man? And if the latter, as was the case, what does this tell us about God and man? It tells us that God's intention in creation will be carried out whether or not particular men freely choose to reject God or to follow His commands. The order of redemption is nothing less than the Godhead being and knowing what it is in the freedom in man while he is actually deciding to choose himself over God.

The response of God will not, however, introduce necessity or coercion into the world as a means to restore this

[3] See Robert Sokolowski, *The God of Faith and Reason* (Washington: Catholic University of America Press, 1995).

order. Herein lies the great redemptive mystery. Man cannot, even in metaphysical terms, be redeemed totally apart from his own free input. Order can be restored only by something other than divine justice, something in the order of a greater freedom or a greater love. This conclusion is the import of the remarkable comment in John Paul II's final book, *Memory and Identity*, in which he maintained that the "divine mercy" stands at the limits of evil.[4] Evil is not absolute. It is limited by that which alone can repair it in its own order, the order of freedom in which alone evil is possible.

But this same divine mercy needed to be manifest in our world to those who needed to know its dimensions. In classical literature, the notion of sacrifice of one's life for a friend is well known. Aristotle speaks of this idea in his discussion of friendship in the *Ethics*. The redemptive theme of laying down one's life for one's friends—"greater love than this no man hath"—was precisely what was taken up and expanded in the Redemption that did take place in historical time. It still constitutes its core. This sacrifice of one's life for one's friends constitutes the final appeal of the good to freedom's risk and decision. The only way we can undo, as it were, a bad choice is by another choice for which we need to have the motive and understanding to so choose. This motive and understanding are supplied by the Redemption—not by some "theory", but by a single life in all its drama. This specific Redemption is only because of the existential status of He who underwent the drama that did take place in human history, human time, when Pontius Pilate, a Roman, was governor in Jerusalem.

[4] John Paul II, *Mystery and Identity* (New York: Rizzoli, 2005), chap. 2.

III

Saint Augustine, in a famous phrase, explained that peace was the "tranquillity of order". Augustine knew the ambiguities of the word *pax*. Imposed order could be a devastation having none of the elements of voluntariness in what is imposed. Tyrannies have their own order, as Plato showed in the ninth book of the *Republic* (chapter 5). Ruin and destruction too have some sort of order. So the order from which tranquillity stems is not a destruction, to recall the famous comment of Tacitus about peace. The parts cannot be the parts unless the whole is the whole. Order does not mean absorbing all the parts into an undifferentiated unity, into a sameness. Rather, it means keeping the parts to be what they are, yet parts that are complete, not intended to be other than they are.

When we die, whether we be saved or damned, we are not ultimately absorbed, disappearing into God. We remain what we are, from our beginning. In salvation, we do not lose our identity. In fact, salvation is precisely the claim that our identity abides. This is, ultimately, the significance of the resurrection of the body. We are not pantheists, who believe everything is God. God, being what He is, keeps us what we are, finite human beings. Indeed, we are particular human beings; each, no matter how much we look like one another, is like unto nothing ever known before or nothing ever to be known again. We remain, we abide, even in our personal uniqueness.

The scandal of the Incarnation, the immediate locus of redemption, is not that man is absorbed into God, but that "the Word was made flesh and dwelt amongst us." That God became true man to redeem us is perhaps what men find most difficult to believe about Christian doctrine.

"This chief mystery of our holy faith", John Henry Newman wrote,

> is the humiliation of the Son of God to temptation and suffering.... In truth, it is a more overwhelming mystery even than that which is involved in the doctrine of the Trinity. I say, more overwhelming, not greater—for we cannot measure the more and less in subjects utterly incomprehensible and divine, but with more in it to perplex and subdue our minds. When the mystery of the Trinity is set before us, we see indeed that it is quite beyond our reason.... But the mystery of the Incarnation relates, in part, to subjects more level with our reason; it lies not only in the manner how God and man is one Christ, but in the very fact that so it is.[5]

The "greater" mystery is the Trinity; the most "overwhelming" mystery is that one Person of this same Trinity actually became man while remaining in His Person true God.

God has His own internal order. God is revealed to us, by this same Son made man, as the Trinity. Benedict XVI succinctly stated the implications of this understanding. The Trinity tells us that

> in the light of the Paschal Mystery is fully revealed the center of the universe and of history. God himself, is eternal and infinite Love.... Love is always a mystery, a reality that surpasses reason, without contradicting it, and more than that, exalts its possibilities. Jesus revealed to us the mystery of God. He, the Son, made us know the Father who is in Heaven, and gave us the Holy Spirit, the Love

[5] John Henry Newman, "The Humiliation of the Eternal Son", in *Parochial and Plain Sermons* (San Francisco: Ignatius Press, [1891] 1997), bk. 3, ser. 12, 583.

> of the Father and of the Son. Christian theology synthesizes the truth of God with this expression: only one substance in three persons. God is not solitude but perfect communion. For this reason the human person, the image of God, realizes himself or herself in love, which is a sincere gift of self.[6]

This understanding of the Trinity, as we have seen, is the premise for understanding the Redemption. The "center of the universe [cosmos] and history" is found in the inner life of the Godhead, which is trinitarian. God is not alone. Since He is perfect communion and we are made in His image, our own being is revealed in the gift of self that is called love. In giving ourselves, we do not lose, but gain, ourselves.

What is not God has its own order, essentially related to the inner life of God as its ultimate source and center. We are promised precisely "eternal life", the inner life of God as our own contemplative end, but also as the primary purpose of creation in the first place. Everything in us and about us is ordained to our achieving this end, even (ironically) our sins, if we would let them. Any lesser understanding of our being seeks the meaning of what we are under false assumptions. We cannot, and do not, except briefly, rest in what is not God. Whatever alternative we choose, however good, will soon exhaust itself and send us elsewhere. We cannot find anything that does not originate in God. Each tiny thing that we encounter, especially each human person, is directly related to the Godhead in all its glory.

[6] Benedict XVI, "Mystery of the Trinity", *L'Osservatore Romano*, May 25, 2005.

IV

C. S. Lewis remarked that we have never met a mere "mortal". Our lives are not insignificant. They are risks. They always stand at the point that divides salvation and damnation. We really can lose our souls. Augustine thought that probably most people in fact did lose them, but only because they chose to reject what was given to them to save them. We like to be optimistic and suggest that no one loses his soul (chapter 7). But if this alternative that no one can lose his soul—that is, do something of such far-reaching consequence—is the fact, it is hard to see how anything is of much importance. If nothing we do, say, or believe can really make any ultimate difference, what is our dignity? On this hypothesis, we end up doing what we want with impunity, but nothing matters anyhow. Surely this insignificance of our thoughts and deeds is not the order of God for our good.

In God's intention, creation did not come first, then men. Men—that is, God's intention to create them—came first, then the rest of creation. We should not allow the immense size of space or its presumed age to lessen the grandeur of spirit. We are given dominion over creation, not it over us, though many ecology movements of recent decades would have it otherwise. We are to order nature for our ends, not denying what it is. But our ends are already placed within us to orient us to what can only be our purpose in existence. "Thou hast made us for Thyself", Augustine said. Nature and animals ought to be better in their own order because of our stewardship. God does not "need" us. God was not once upon a time unhappy, then, with some surprise, found us wandering about the planet Earth, offering Him our friendship. God was always happy, complete. The human being that did not make itself cannot explain himself by himself. The order of human being is not first its own self-made order.

Our order is greater than we could propose for ourselves. This is why it is not ours to establish in the first place. *Sapientis est ordinare.* The end of all things is not that we establish here a lasting city of our own composition, even though we have cities and we are to rule them. The end of all things is that, having been first chosen, we still must choose—choose not ourselves, but eternal life within the conditions in which it is offered to us. And we do this implicitly in our relation to others, in our gifts of ourselves. But this end is also offered to us so that it itself falls in the order of our freedom, almost as if it would be impossible to complete the plan or order of redemption without our cooperation.

Before anything begins, God *is.* That is, God stands outside of nothingness. God is all-complete, existing with an inner trinitarian life that needs no world, no man, no angel. If anything but God exists, it is not because something is deficient or lonely in God. What is not God cannot explain itself to itself without God. *God's purpose in creation is to associate other knowing beings, angels and men, in His inner life.* This purpose never changes. No "natural" angelic or human condition ever in fact existed, even though it might have.

That is, both angels and men were, from the beginning, intended to be more than their nature allowed them to expect by their own good but limited being. *Homo non proprie humanus sed superhumanus est.* This race of men to which we belong has a supernatural end, no other. For their own good, as it were, men are given another choice. This elevated condition, however, was not "due" to man or angel but was given in order that the primary end of creation, participation in the inner life of the Godhead, be realized.

The cosmos finds its purpose through its relation to the initial design of God in inviting rational beings into His inner, trinitarian life. Even though the cosmos comes first in time, it does not come first in the divine intention. God could not, however, simply associate free beings with Himself apart from the dynamics of their free being. As we noted of Plato in the *Symposium*, the universe seemed to need, for its own perfection, free creatures, beings who could appreciate it. The free creature can reject that for which it exists, but he can also choose it. This was the risk of God.

The Fall is the account of free creatures' claiming themselves to be the cause of the order and nature of things, particularly their own order. The essential temptation is for oneself, not God, to be the cause of the distinction between good and evil. This is what Genesis is about. God's only choice, to avoid this unpleasant possibility of free beings choosing to reject His order, would be not to create at all, so that nothing but God would exist. As such, this alternative would not be a bad thing. God would commit no evil in not creating. Yet something in the goodness of God seeks to diffuse itself, not of necessity, but out of delight, out of joy in giving what is good and seeing creatures' happiness. The greater good was that joy could exist even if some might reject its order of coming to be. This aspect of goodness is what lies at the origin of our being and that of creation.

Evidently, from the beginning, the First Parents, like the angels, were themselves intended for the initial purpose of God in creation. They were not simply "natural" human beings. Had they definitively not sinned, their destiny would have been the elevated relation to the inner life of God that is promised to all rational creation after their own capacities. We do not know how this would have worked. What changed with the Fall of both angels and men was not the ultimate end for which human beings were created, but rather the means whereby, granted the free rejection by men and angels of God's initial plan, this end could still be achieved in all its integrity.

Revelation, through the promises to Israel and the Incarnation, and through both to the Church and all the nations, did not change the end for which God created in the first place. It did change the means by which that purpose was to be achieved. Man would now be saved, as even the Greeks suspected, by suffering. The Incarnation and Redemption restored to man a definite way of reaching the original end for which he was created, but this way would now lead through death.

The Redemption did not, however, restore the elevated gifts, especially that of not dying, that were given to the original human beings. This lack of what might have been does not mean that no alternate gifts were to be forthcoming. In John's prologue, we read the phrase "grace upon grace". The order of redemption is one aware of this "grace upon grace" that we are given through the Incarnation and Nativity, through the actual appearance of the Word made flesh in this world and the drama that ensued from this appearance.

Of course, God understood that the Fall both could and would happen, but His knowing did not cause it. His knowledge in fact could not have *not* known this possibility. It is intrinsic in the knowledge of what a free being is and is possible to it. The cause lies in the will and loves of the free creature. The Incarnation and Redemption, the Cross and Resurrection, are the way that human beings are to return to God's initial purpose. The *felix culpa* does imply that the Incarnation, in the way we know it, is the surprising, almost shocking, response of God to our freedom.

We would like, perhaps, to think of some "gentler" way whereby we could freely reach the end for which we exist. But the particular Incarnation and Redemption that we know in revelation and is described in Scripture teach us both the terrible consequences of sin and the extraordinary free glory into which we are invited in God's initial purpose. It also teaches us that our redemption was primarily and essentially achieved by Christ's suffering and death, by His leaving to us the Memorial of this death as the central way to worship God, something that mankind has been persistently searching for from the beginning.

The original plan of God in creation is being worked out in history. Our unique lives are immersed in this very working out. The most important thing in history is that we each achieve the end for which we are created. This end is offered to everyone, and as John Paul II often said, God does not deny the means for those of good will who seek. But all of this possibility is dependent on the Incarnation and the Redemption through Church and sacrament that Christ has revealed to be the way back to our end.

This end is to live eternal life beholding, delighting in the inner life of God in the company of all beings who choose to accept this end, an acceptance that no one can achieve without grace and personal choice. On the other hand, it includes what is the most amazing part of the whole salvific effort looked at from the human individual's point of view, namely, that the resurrection of the body, hence the completeness of his individual personality, is essential to the end of creation. What we would actually want if we could have it is in fact the truth of the order of redemption.

V

The effort to understand more completely what has been revealed is a central and common Catholic position. Love, as Benedict XVI said in speaking of the Trinity, exalts the "possibilities of reason". In an earlier lecture given in Spain, Joseph Cardinal Ratzinger (later to become Pope Benedict XVI) explained that theology begins and must begin not from what the philosopher devises but from what is handed down.

> If theology wishes [to be] and should be something other than religious studies, other than occupying ourselves with ever unsolved questions concerning what is greater than ourselves and nonetheless makes us what we are, then it can only be based on starting from an answer that we ourselves have not devised; yet in order for this to become a real answer for us, we have to try to understand it, not to resolve it. That is what is peculiar to theology, that it turns to something we ourselves have not devised and that is able to be the foundation of our life, in that it goes before us and supports us; that is to say, it is greater than our own thought.[7]

Philosophy is what the theologian uses to explain, or make clearer to us, what is found in revelation. Revelation is also addressed to our intelligence. Intelligence seeks to see the order in things, including the things handed down, the things we did not "devise". It is the task of philosophy to examine "unresolved questions concerning what is greater than ourselves" and to compare these analyses with one another while not neglecting the claims of revelation as themselves indicating their own order.

[7] Joseph Cardinal Ratzinger, *Pilgrim Fellowship of Faith: The Church as Communion* (San Francisco: Ignatius Press, 2005), 31.

We did not "devise" the way we are to be redeemed or saved. Events happened in Bethlehem, Nazareth, and Jerusalem. They are recorded, handed down, and testified to. But on the way to revelation's directing the way we are to live, we need to understand and to defend ourselves from views that would obscure or deny what is revealed. One of the earliest "intellectuals" to become a prominent member of the developing Church was a philosopher known as Justin Martyr in the early second century A.D. We have left to us an account of his trial and martyrdom under a Roman prefect by the name of Rusticus. Significantly enough, the emperor at the time of his execution was the famous philosopher-emperor Marcus Aurelius, whose Stoic *Meditations* are still well worth reading. We have here a renewal of that conflict between polity, revelation, and philosophy that has its origins in the trials of Socrates and Christ.

In the legal framework of the trial, Justin presents us with a vivid account of his understanding of what he stood for and what he is on trial for, a position evidently against the civil law at the time. Thus, there is already a conflict between obeying God and obeying Caesar. Justin was asked to deny what he and the other martyrs held or else be beheaded. In the process, he made the following statement that gives us some indication of the priorities within the order of redemption as this order is handed down.

> [We] worship the God of the Christians. We hold him to be from the beginning the one creator and maker of the whole creation, of things seen and things unseen. We worship also the Lord Jesus Christ, the Son of God. He was foretold by the prophets as the future herald of salvation for the human race and the teacher of distinguished disciples. For myself, since I am a human being, I consider

> that what I say is insignificant in comparison with his infinite godhead.[8]

Justin is not "devising" his own theory. But he tells us what he holds in words that are already resonant with great creeds written after his time. God is the maker of the cosmos. Christ is his Son. Christ was foretold by the prophets. He is sent for the salvation of the human race. He is a teacher of the truth. But still, Justin makes intelligible to Rusticus, the governor, what he holds. Both Rusticus and Justin think what we hold makes a difference. Justin is executed by the Roman state because he is a witness to what Christ taught. He is not surprised that he is to follow the model of Christ, the Cross. He does not rebel or complain that some other, perhaps easier or more rational, way is not open to him.

By the order of redemption, then, we mean something other than the way of the philosophers, who have honorably striven to figure out other ways to explain our lot, ways that often contain much truth. But they have not arrived by themselves at the way Justin indicates. It is not that no point of contact exists between politician, philosopher, and believer, even though as Saint Paul would point out, the way of Christ crucified was a scandal to the Jews and foolishness to the Greeks. We are asked to see that this "scandal" and this "foolishness" are in fact responses to the fallen condition of men in a final divine effort to save those who will be saved. To be saved means, in Christian terms, literally to find favor with God by obeying and following His commands as they are found explicated in the life of Christ. These ways are to be found preserved and handed down in the Church, which is responsible for keeping them

[8] *The Liturgy of the Hours*, Feast of St. Justin, June 1, Office of Readings.

and passing them down. When we find them, it is a delight, not a burden, unless we see only our own version of salvation and not the one given to us.

The order of redemption implies a certain overturning of values—not exactly a rejection of the natural virtues, but a going beyond them in a way that seems to make them more what they are. At the center of the order of redemption is innocent suffering taken on by the Son of God not for suffering's sake but for the sake of turning our wills to what is the right order of things. This right understanding includes a realization of why we exist in this particular order that includes the Fall. Revelation contains within itself, however, not only an understanding of what we are, what God is, and what the world is, but also of what we ought to do. Revelation is not primarily a system of morality, but it implies and demands one. It is not ashamed to learn from the philosophers. It is premised on the fact that our first duty is to love God, and to love our neighbor as a consequence of the first.

What this latter love of neighbor implies is seen in its most noble form of laying down one's life for one's friends, not merely in death but in everyday life. This is why justice is seen in terms primarily of service. That is, all the virtues become related to the new life so that all virtues become more what they are. It is clear, however, that since we are loved by a more-than-human love for a more-than-human end, and we are ourselves to love in this way, we need what is called "grace" to accomplish our end. This grace is promised to us in abundance but also is intrinsic to the proper worship of God that is contained in revelation, which no longer leaves us free to worship God in any way we please. Again, this is conceived as a freedom and a glory, something we want to know when we do not know it.

"The grace promised us is given, not that we may know more, but that we may do better. It is given to influence, guide, and strengthen us in performing our duty towards God and man", Newman writes.

> It is given to us as creatures, as sinners, as men, as immortal beings, not as mere reasoners, disputers, or philosophical inquirers. It teaches what we are, whither we are going, what we must do, how we must do it; it enables us to change our fallen nature from evil to good.... But it tells us nothing for the *sake* of telling it; neither in His Holy Word, nor through our consciences, has the Blessed Spirit thought fit to act. Not that the desire of knowing sacred things for the sake of knowing them is wrong.[9]

These are striking phrases—we are given graces not as "reasoners, disputers, or philosophical inquirers", yet there is nothing as such wrong with such inquiries. Indeed, looked at in a broader way, these natural intellectual virtues may be an essential aspect of our existence and prepare us for what is revealed.

But what Newman was getting at here is that Christianity may not be a formula for a worldly success by its practitioners if they adhere to its commandments. It may in fact seem like foolishness, and it may be—and is—persecuted, even today, for being what it is. The modern temptation has always been to demand of Christianity that, to be believable, it produce an inner-worldly order whereby man could find the complete explanation of himself in this world and its politics, not by way of the Cross but by way of the world. What has been under attack has

[9] John Henry Newman, "The Christian Mysteries", in *Parochial and Plain Sermons*, bk. 1, ser. 16, 131.

been not so much doctrine as practice. That is, the second commandment, about love of neighbor, has taken a certain definite authority over the first commandment of worshipping God above all things. What has happened is that certain ideological concepts of what the world should be, from liberalism to socialism, even to Islam, become themselves criteria for judging whether Christianity is a "success" in the world.

Christianity finds itself, in a way, caught between two very different criteria. Within the order of redemption is already also found an account of how to live bound up with our duty to God. The accusation that by observing its duty to God Christianity thereby neglects or obviates any duty to man in terms of the orders of the world is both an ancient and a modern one. It is quite true that the admonitions of how to live are to be observed no matter what the political order, though some political orders are more conducive than others.

But it is not clear in practice that prosperity and peace are always a better place to save our souls than poverty and turmoil. Indeed, poverty seems to be more favored by the Christian teaching on the poor. In any case, within Christianity there is found a doctrine on how to live that seems to be central to its teaching. The criteria given at the final Judgment are mostly ones of relation to others—feeding the hungry, turning the other cheek, even sacrificing one's life for one's friends, though in other places we are admonished also to know the truth to be free.

Thus, the order of redemption is itself also, in its own understanding of itself, directed both to practice and to knowing. We are both to "confess" what we hold, even before the nations, and to be concerned for and love our neighbor in a practical way, even to the point of creating a culture in which we can live well. The natural virtues are not to be unknown or neglected, but they are to be seen also in the light of faith, hope, and charity so that something more is expected of us than what is minimally fair or just. This combination of practice and knowledge takes us back to our initial observation that the purpose of God will be achieved within the world in whatever regime or era in which we find ourselves, even the worst.

Moreover, the primacy of the Cross in Christianity takes us back to the primary Socratic principle that "it is better to suffer evil than to do it." This principle is reaffirmed and deepened by the Cross. Socrates would not do evil, so he suffered, rather cheerfully, the consequences of his refusal. He drank the hemlock, that is, was executed by the state. In doing so, he upheld the principle.

Christ's crucifixion subsumes Socrates. Both Christ and Socrates are innocent of the crimes attributed to them. Socrates is a philosopher who upholds a basic principle. Christ is the God-man executed by men. He not only upholds the same principle but voluntarily does the will of His Father in so suffering. Because of His sacrifice, He restores the alienation of man from God so that sins are forgiven and the way to the original purpose of creation—the association of free creatures in the Godhead—is open, though it still must be chosen after the manner of Christ's teachings and example.

The principle that it is never right to do wrong is upheld by both the deaths of Christ and Socrates. This same principle, as it were, also has an "intellectual" component as one that manifests itself in action. It is wrong, morally and intellectually wrong, to affirm that something that is in fact evil is good. It is even worse to teach it or to establish laws to enforce it. It is not merely that we should not do what is evil, but we should not affirm it, stand for it, or justify it. Revelation presupposes a certain congruity between action and mind even in the things revealed to us, perhaps especially in the things revealed to us.

The fact is that if we do not understand, accept, and, yes, practice the teachings we find in the order of redemption in which we live, we will seek to justify our lives and deeds with another theory. We will formulate and practice another account of reality that does not adhere to those unchangeable truths that are set down in the tradition and explored by the mind reflecting on it. Philosophy, in this sense, when it is not rooted in *what is*, can be harmful to us, not merely "foolishness".

In the end, however, we recall that Christ came into the world not to call the saved, but sinners (Mt 9:13). What this actual order of redemption implies is that the world was to be allowed to go on in its basic struggle that is found in our souls about whether we will accept redemption as a gift through the sacrifice of Christ. We will not find an age or a nation or a class in which the problem of sinners does not appear. Christ did not fail because such sin has continued relatively unabated over the centuries since the Incarnation. Nothing otherwise was ever promised.

Indeed, the constant appearance of sin and evil was predicted, as was the sole way in which it could be combated, by suffering understood as the refusal to do evil or to define evil as good. The ultimate things would not be finally sorted out in this life, but they would be sorted out eventually. The order of redemption leads to a final Judgment in which the difference between those who choose good and evil is finally and permanently established. This is the teaching of Christ's Redemption. It alone frees us from the constantly recurring enterprises of discovering alternate redemptions and salvations composed of our own theories and desires. Redemption teaches us that error is not merely a missing of the mark but leads inevitably to the erection of a counter kingdom in which we ourselves, not the Cross, are at the center.

We can conclude with the final words of Newman's sermon "The Humiliation of the Eternal Son", a sermon we have already cited:

> May God, even the Father, give us a heart and understanding to realize, as well as to confess that doctrine into which we were baptized, that His Only-begotten Son, our Lord, was conceived by the Holy Ghost, was born of the Virgin Mary, suffered, and was buried, rose again from the dead, ascended into heaven, from whence He shall come again, at the end of the world to judge the quick and the dead![10]

This is as brief and succinct a statement of the order of redemption that we can find, a doctrine that we are both to "understand" and "confess".

[10] Newman, "The Humiliation of the Eternal Son", in ibid. bk. 3, ser. 12, 592–93.

CHAPTER IX

THE ORDER OF BEAUTY

Omne ens est pulchrum (Every being is beautiful).

—Thomas Aquinas

Beatrice is to be loved because she is beautiful; but she is beautiful because there is behind her a many-sided mystery of beauty, to be seen also in the grass and the sea, and even in the dead gods. There is a promise in and yet beyond all such pictures.

—G. K. Chesterton, *Illustrated London News*, March 22, 1930

"Aquinas", said Stephen, "says that is beautiful the apprehension of which pleases." Lynch nodded. "I remember that, he said, *Pulchra sunt quae visa placent.*" "He uses the word *visa*", said Stephen, "to cover esthetic apprehensions of all kinds, whether through sight or hearing or through any other avenue of apprehension. . . . Plato, I believe, said that beauty is the splendour of truth. I don't think that it has a meaning, but the true and the beautiful are akin. Truth is beheld by the intellect which is appeased by the most satisfying relations of the intelligible; beauty is beheld by the imagination which is appeased by the most satisfying relation of the sensible."

—James Joyce, *Portrait of the Artist as a Young Man*, chap. 5

I

On Tuesday, March 31, 1772, Boswell records that several friends were dining at General Paoli's. At one point the question came up about whether there was such a thing as beauty independent of utility. Evidently, the General maintained that there was not any such independence. To this observation, Samuel Johnson insisted that there was a difference. To illustrate his position, he pointed to a coffee cup that he held in his hand. He indicated that "the painting on [this cup] was of no real use, as the cup would hold the coffee equally well if plain, yet the painting was beautiful." [1] The point of this initial way to begin to talk of the order of beauty is not that useful things cannot also be beautiful, but that what the beautiful adds to usefulness is not necessarily something more useful, but something that is beyond utility. The highest things among us, including what is beautiful, are precisely "beyond utility".

A friend of mine and his wife recently had a baby girl, their fourth child. When the new daughter was about two months old, I was talking to my friend on the phone about how the older children (from four to eleven) were taking to the new baby. He replied, in some astonishment, "I have never seen anything so beautiful in my life." Notice that this description does not refer to either the new daughter herself (who is very lovely) or to the older children. Rather, it indicates something less tangible. It refers, namely, to seeing how the older children responded to the little daughter. It was their very welcoming or enjoyment of the new little sister, with her reaction to them, that struck the father. This reaction was almost something outside of his control,

[1] *Boswell's Life of Johnson* (London: Oxford, 1931), 1:449.

yet it was something he observed as it happened and in which he himself rejoiced as actively delighting in the scene.

A third, not dissimilar, introductory incident I wish to recall here. A number of years ago, Ignatius Press published a book of mine entitled *Idylls and Rambles*. In this collection of short essays was one entitled "Radiance". It recalls an incident that goes back perhaps thirty years or so. One Sunday, I happened to be visiting friends in Trenton, New Jersey. I concelebrated Mass that morning in the parish my friends had attended as youngsters, a famous and beautiful old church. When the Mass was over, a number of baptisms of children followed, as is usual in a big parish. After leaving the sacristy to meet the friends with whom I was staying, I happened to pass by the baptistery, where a couple with surrounding family were gathered for the baptism of their child.

Here, I will cite what I recorded years ago, because it makes a point about beauty that will be a major part of our consideration of what I will call here the "order of beauty." The classical definition of beauty, as we see recalled in the Joyce passage, is "that which, when seen, pleases". The word "pleases" is perhaps too mild, though it is accurate. Here follow my remarks on this incident in Trenton:

> I went over briefly to see more closely the first baby as the parents brought her up to the baptismal font.... She was dressed in white, with a cute bonnet. Her mother told me, if I recall correctly, that her name was Emily, a name I quite like. She was maybe a month old, and I touched her head just to prove again, mainly to myself, that anything so dear could be real. She was an absolutely radiant child. She rather took my breath away—I was merely walking by on the way to the front door of the church, quite unprepared to glimpse such unexpected beauty, though I have come to realize that

> beauty is always unexpected. We realize, I think, that the vivid beauty and innocence of the human child do not come from us, even if we be its parents.[2]

Recently, I told the above story of the father's account of the reaction of his three children to the new baby sister to an ex-student, now in medical school. I told her that the incident reminded me of the "Radiance" essay and asked if she had ever seen that essay. She replied immediately, "The little girl's name was Emily."

Thus far, we see that beauty has a classical definition. It is not utility, but it is not opposed to it either. Useful things, products of our hands and our practical intellects, can also be beautiful and indeed perhaps should be. Beauty pleases, yet it also can take our breath away. Somehow, it "radiates". It has a splendor. There is a reality about it that is truly there, a reality that we acknowledge and react to. Beauty applies to and arises within the being that possesses it. It is related to the truth of things. Being itself, as Chesterton noticed, reveals more than itself, almost as if the beauty we see or hear or touch could not cause itself, even when we are involved in its coming to be, as in the painting on the cup that Johnson saw. Beauty is related to the sensible. We react to it. But it is comprehended too, almost as if it were light. Intellectual light also shines through what is beautiful. We are struck by it; we remember it.

A final initial comment with regard to beauty relates to an essay entitled "What Is a Classic?" of the South African novelist J. M. Coetzee. He recalls one Sunday afternoon in Cape Town in the summer of 1955. He was fifteen years old. He was bored, "the main problem of existence in those

[2] *Idylls and Rambles: Lighter Christian Essays* (San Francisco: Ignatius Press, 1994), 54.

days", with nothing much to do. He was in the back garden of his parents' home. Suddenly, he says, "From the house next door I heard music. As long as the music lasted, I was frozen, I dared not breathe. I was being spoken to by the music as music had never spoken to me before."

Coetzee at the time knew or cared little about music. The music was Bach's *Well-Tempered Clavier*, as he found out later. After hearing this music, he tells us, "Everything changed." He adds, "Bach thinks in music. Music thinks itself in Bach."[3] The beautiful "freezes" us when we hear it. We listen to it knowing that it is also something of the mind. It can strike us at any time or place, even in a backyard in Cape Town or while dining at General Paoli's. It has the power, on encountering it, of unsettling our very world that we thought was complete.

The beautiful is a sign of our human finiteness. It is part of our glory that we can be receptive to what is not of ourselves yet is somehow still addressed to us. The fact that the same beautiful music can also strike us yesterday afternoon does not take away from its striking a fifteen-year-old boy in South Africa in 1955. Beauty has the astonishing character of coming to us from outside of our anticipation of it. It is a sign of what is greater than ourselves, without denying that we are somehow oriented to it.

II

No doubt, in Christian literature, the most commonly read and most famous passage about beauty is found in the

[3] J. M. Coetzee, "What Is a Classic?" *Stranger Stories: Literary Essays* (Harmondsworth: Penguin, 2001), 8–9.

Confessions of Saint Augustine (bk. 10, no. 27). In the background of Augustine is surely, besides Scripture, both the Greek philosophers Plato and Plotinus. They remind us that the perplexity of beauty—what it is, its inner order, its capacity to strike us on beholding it—are things that have arisen among our kind almost from the beginning.

Plotinus, for instance, who lived in the third century A.D., remarked in his *Enneads* that

> beauty addresses itself chiefly to sight; but there is a beauty from the hearing too, as in certain combinations of words and in all kinds of music, for melodies and cadences are beautiful; and minds that lift themselves above the realm of sense to a high order are aware of beauty in the conduct of life, in actions, in character, in the pursuits of the intellect; and there is the beauty of the virtues. (1, 6, 1)

Plotinus then added, enigmatically, something that catches our curiosity even more. "What loftier beauty there may yet be, our argument will bring to light." We see here not only the attention to music that we found in the Coetzee incident in Cape Town, but a realization that beauty can apply to virtue or even to knowledge. The music of Bach also attracts our mind. What is it, this beauty that puzzles us?

Joseph Cardinal Ratzinger, in his *Spirit of the Liturgy*, touched on this same point about Bach, and added Mozart: "Whether it is Bach or Mozart that we hear in church, we have a sense in either case of what the *gloria Dei*, the glory of God, means. The mystery of infinite beauty is there and enables us to experience the presence of God more truly and vividly than in many sermons."[4] The "mystery of

[4] Joseph Cardinal Ratzinger, *The Spirit of the Liturgy* (San Francisco: Ignatius Press, 2000), 146.

infinite beauty" is found expressed in the music—not merely in an abstraction or a theory, but as something experienced in listening to the music itself. The very word "glory" indicates a burgeoning beauty that seems to transcend its finite expression.

Implicit in Plotinus' reflections is also a progression, as if one beautiful thing implies another, even an origin. We saw this aspect in the Chesterton comment as well as in the music of Bach and Mozart. Later on in the *Enneads*, Plotinius asks, using a word clearly related to beauty, "What is love?" He recalls Plato on this topic: "Now everyone recognizes that the emotional state for which we make this 'Love' responsible rises in souls aspiring to be knit in the closest union with some beautiful object." Plotinus notices that this love can be abused; that is, it has a proper order to be what it is. However, "the primal source of Love is a tendency of the Soul towards pure beauty." All real and finite love seems to live in the shadow of a pure beauty it does not immediately encounter.

Plotinus adds, "Pure Love seeks beauty alone, whether there is reminiscence or not; but there are those that feel, also, a desire of such immortality as lies within mortal reach; and these are seeking beauty in their demand for perpetuity, the desire of the eternal" (3, 5, 1). In this passage, we find that aspect of Greek biology that saw in begetting on the part of any species, including the human one, a search for its own immortality. Individuals needed to exist, of course, if the species were to exist. Without denying this collective aspect of the question, Christians were prodded, no doubt because of the doctrine of the Resurrection of the body, to wonder not merely about the species, the existence of which was in fact an abstraction, but about the immortality and even more about the resurrection of the whole person. This wonder was seen to be implicit in the notion of beauty and why the nostalgic notion of "fading beauty", whether of flowers or of human beings, brought forth such a poignancy since the "fadingness" seemed to be contrary to what was implicit in beauty as such.

In his marvelous treatment of Plato's *Phaedrus*, Josef Pieper points out that Plato was aware that man was not in himself complete by his own self-making. "Real man", Pieper wrote, "is a being by nature given to shattering emotion. A good deed is better for having been committed with passion."[5] What Pieper intends to show here is that beauty has the everyday capacity of breaking into our seemingly closed world from the most unexpected human, natural, and even supernatural sources. It can shatter our presumed completeness or merely remind us of the narrowness of our understanding of ordinary things.

Some twenty years ago, as an instance of this latter ordinary incident, I happened to be at the Missouri State Fair at Sedelia. State fairs are often showcases for the agricultural production of the state. Missouri is famous for its mules. While I had seen mules before, they always appeared to me to be a rather awkward and ungainly sort of animal, existing as close to the "practical" or the "useful" as any animal could be. It was easy to think, as the very names indicate, that we do not look to a donkey or jackass for beauty.

At this fair, however, there was a display of the best mules in Missouri, which were, ipso facto, the best mules in the world. When I walked into the show barn where the judging of the mules was taking place, I was almost dumbfounded to see the beauty of these brown, black, and white creatures.

[5] Josef Pieper, *Enthusiasm and the Divine Madness: On the Platonic Dialogue* Phaedrus (New York: Harcourt, 1964), 22.

I had never thought a mule could be described as "beautiful". But there they were, lots of them. Had they been thoroughbred horses in Lexington, Kentucky, I would not have been nearly so struck, since I would expect the striking beauty of thoroughbreds. I had, of course, seen beautiful dogs and cats, foxes, rabbits, and lions, even cattle, but never a beautiful mule. The experience made me realize that beauty can happen, if we know how to see or hear it, in any category of being. As Aquinas said, "Every being is beautiful."

But to return to Pieper's point, he was concerned to emphasize that we ought to be moved in our whole being by what is beautiful. The opposite thesis had been argued by Lysias, who wanted to make love and beauty salable items. Plato would have none of this. Plato has "a portrait of a soul which receives into its depths the emotion aroused by sensuous beauty, and simultaneously renounces physical gratification of that beauty."[6] Plotinus seems to have followed Plato on this point, which is that beauty is another aspect of being than is the good.

It is possible and part of the perfection of our nature that beauty is simply what pleases us, what crashes into our world to remind us of how incomplete it is if we simply rely on our own making. Something of this same experience is recorded in Genesis when Adam cannot find a companion of his own flesh among the other animals and beings that God has created. On seeing Eve for the first time, he recognizes something new brought into his world. He is struck by the congruity and yet the difference that she represents.

At the end of the *Phaedrus*, we find a passage of remarkable import. Socrates and Phaedrus have realized that the best we human beings can do is not to be called "wise",

[6] Ibid., 21.

but only "lovers of wisdom"—the literal meaning of the word "philosopher". We need a certain poetic or transcendent inspiration to claim a title to anything more. This insight would become, later on, embodied in the notion of grace among the Christians. But philosophers understand that "nature has placed the love of wisdom in our minds" when we realize that lesser things no longer satisfy us and that we are led by a "divine impulse . . . to more important things".

At this point, Socrates proposes perhaps the most lovely pagan prayer ever written, as something to be said at the end of their conversation at this charming spot. It reads, "O dear Pan and all the other gods of this place, grant that I may be beautiful inside. Let all my external possessions be in friendly harmony with what is within. May I consider the wise man rich. And as for gold, let me have as much as a moderate man could bear and carry with him" (279b–c).

Such a passage reminds us that physical beauty, however lovely it is, can obscure to us the beauties of souls that shine through on the countenance of those we see. Our "inside" and our "outside", as it were, should reveal each other. Wendell Berry touched on this point in his essay "The Body and the Earth". We have set up spurious "models" of what we ought to look like, Berry wrote, and if we deviate from these models, we suffer in our self-image, even if we in fact be beautiful and attractive by other standards. "Girls are taught to want to be leggy, slender, large-breasted, curly-haired, unimposingly beautiful", Berry observed. "Boys are instructed to be 'athletic' in build, tall but not too tall, broad-shouldered, deep-chested, narrow-hipped, square-jawed, straight-nosed, not bald, unimposingly handsome."[7]

[7] Wendell Berry, "The Body and the Earth", in *Recollected Essays, 1965–1980* (New York: Farrar, Straus and Giroux, 1998), 288.

The trouble with such "models", Berry thinks, is that they obscure even from ourselves the beauty of a greater depth. "Though many people, in health, are beautiful," he continues, "very few resemble these models. . . . Woe, above all, to the woman with small breasts or a muscular body or strong features. Homer and Solomon might have thought her beautiful, but she will see her own beauty only by a difficult rebellion." The beauty that Plato especially warned us that would come crashing into our world was precisely this deeper beauty that Berry had in mind. But no philosopher ever doubts that the beautiful has manifestations in our physical being, that beauty has an admirable unity, integrity, and radiance about it that does not allow us to deny it. And the fact that beauty is not identical with the good, even though the same being is good and beautiful, reminds us that beauty is primarily to be "beheld", as if it is ours only as a gift, as a reminder of what is more than we are.

A friend told me the story of her eighty-year-old father, who was taking care of her invalid and very aging and ailing mother. The daughter was with her father one day in the nursing home. He took her mother's face in his hands, looked at her for a long time and exclaimed to his daughter, "Isn't she beautiful!" It is of these experiences that the philosophers and prophets speak.

III

Chapter 27 of book 10 of Augustine's *Confessions* returns us to a theme we find in the Platonic corpus. Perhaps no passage quite captures the notion of the order of beautiful things as does this one of Augustine. "Late have I loved Thee, beauty so ancient and so new, late have I loved Thee!" Augustine implicitly here acknowledged that he has not always loved this beauty. He knows that he is late in coming to it. Beauty, moreover, is what calls him, and once Augustine is alerted to its fairness, beauty becomes the object of his desire, becomes a good for him. And the object of his assignation is personal, a "Thou", as in the earlier translations.

In the explanation of how it was that he had missed this beauty earlier in his life, the famous chapter continues,

> For behold you were within me and I was without, and there did I seek you. In my unfair state I rushed heedlessly among the beautiful things of your creation. You were with me, but I was not with you. Those things kept me far from you, though they had no true existence except in you. You called and cried aloud, and forced open my deafness.

Indeed, Augustine proceeds to use images of all the senses—sight, sound, taste, touch, and smell—as if any beauty perceived can lift him to its ultimate origins.

What is particularly striking about this passage is that Augustine does not deny that the things that caused him to turn away from God's beauty were themselves beautiful. The implication is that were they not, he never would have noticed them. He here says again what so many others have noticed: that finite beauty does not explain itself but hints at something beyond itself. It creates its own restlessness. He is concerned not just with an abstract beauty, but with one that has "existence". This sense of reality explains the constant emphasis on tangibility that we find in Augustine.

Another striking idea found in this passage is that Augustine declares that the beauty he is looking for is already in him, not outside of him. He has been looking in the wrong place. But he is not simply seeking himself, as if he were the primary object of his own love. How can this inner discovery of beauty be? He accuses himself of looking elsewhere for it, in "all those beautiful things". But it was within him all along. Augustine is acutely aware of his own reality, his own existence, his finiteness. His is the metaphysics, as Gilson remarked in a famous essay, that finds reality beginning in one's own existence.[8] And this is legitimate, as he is as much real as anything else and has as much need of explaining how and that he is.

Augustine tells us that God opened up his "deafness", but not by denying that finite things were beautiful. We would completely misunderstand Augustine here if we thought that somehow his problem was that he thought finite things not to be themselves also beautiful in their own orders. When he does finally turn to himself, what he finds "inside" is his awareness of his own reality as also something given to him. He is conscious that his own existence, as that of other things, can be properly described as beautiful. But if so, whence did it come? Not from Monica or Patrick, his parents, yet from them also. They need as much explanation as he himself does. They too "had no true existence except in God". It is little wonder that such reflections on his own being give Augustine a clue better to understand the inner life of the Godhead.

IV

The sober lesson of Plato's *Symposium* is that beauty and virtue are to go hand in hand. Beauty is not itself a

[8] Étienne Gilson, "The Future of Augustinian Metaphysics", in *A Monument to St. Augustine* (London: Sheed and Ward, 1945), 287–316.

justification for any action of desire toward its obtaining. In resisting the seductive beauty of Alcibiades, Socrates teaches us that virtue is required to recognize what is really beautiful about someone. As in the case of Alcibiades himself, beauty can corrupt or be made to do so, to use itself as a means to some other end, something Augustine also saw in "all those beautiful things".

The great discussion of Diotima with Socrates on beauty in the *Symposium* is no doubt the classical discussion of the topic. "'Try to pay attention to me,' she said, 'as best you can. You see, the man who has been thus far guided in matters of Love, who has beheld beautiful things in the right order and correctly, is coming now to the goal of Loving: all of a sudden he will catch sight of something wonderfully beautiful in its nature; that, Socrates, is the reason for all his earlier labors'" (210e). Beautiful things must be beheld "in the right order". Knowing the beautiful does not come to us "without labor". Loving has a goal, the "catching sight of something wonderfully beautiful".

"This is what it is to go aright, or to be led by another, into the mystery of Love", Diotima continues her lesson.

> One goes always upwards for the sake of this Beauty, starting out from beautiful things and using them like rising stairs: from one body to two and from two to all beautiful bodies, then from beautiful bodies to beautiful customs, and from customs to learning beautiful things, and from these lessons, he arrives in the end at this lesson, which is learning of this very Beauty, so that in the end he comes to know just what it is to be beautiful. (211b–c)

To do this, Diotima tells Socrates, is "life". That is where we should live. We should "behold that Beauty". It cannot be measured by gold or any other pleasure. This passage again reflects the advice from the prayer in the *Phaedrus*. We need enough gold to survive, but it is not to measure what is beauty. Seeking this beauty is how we should spend our lives, to make our inside conform to what is Beautiful in itself insofar as we can.

One cannot read Plato without becoming aware of that upward thrust that is contained in every beautiful thing. It was something Augustine understood well. It is not intended to deny that many beautiful things exist. Rather, it teaches us that the limited beauty of each thing, once perceived, leaves us with a wonder about how it got this way. At its best this upward drive in beautiful things prevents us from resting in what is beautiful but which is not its origin. In a way, we seek blindly. We wonder if it is possible for us by ourselves to find or confront such a beauty. We suspect that it is not possible. And this is what opens up the drama found in Plato to that found in Augustine, who tells us, when speaking of the Platonists, that they spoke of the Word, but not the Word made flesh.

V

Aquinas' most lengthy treatment of beauty is found in his commentary on the treatise *On The Divine Names* attributed to Dionysus the Areopagite. Again, even in Aquinas, beauty is discussed in a Platonic setting (3, 4, 5–6). Immediately, Aquinas tells us the beauty that we know is a "participated" beauty. That is, it is not explained only in its own terms. "God is said to be super-substantial beauty." Why is God called "beautiful"? Because to all created beings, He gives beauty according to what is due or proper to each. There is a harmony (*consonatia*) and a clarity (*claritas*) in God; that is, the inner life of God has an order to it.

We find a twofold harmony in things, a familiar theme in Aquinas. The first order is according to the order of creatures to God, to Himself as their end. A second form of harmony is said to lie in things according to how they are ordered to each other. Thus all things are ordered to each other insofar as they are all ordered to the same end. God is the font of all beauty. Thus beauty is the principle of all things as their effective cause giving them being. "Beauty which is God is the effective and motive cause." Whatever has its proper beauty, moreover, wishes to multiply it, insofar as possible by communicating something that is similar to it. The existence of "all those beautiful things" of which Augustine spoke is related to something about beauty itself. Far from being selfish and wanting to retain beauty to itself, the Godhead seeks to make *all that is* to be also beautiful.

Beauty and good are the same, because all things desire the beautiful and the good. But they differ because beauty adds above the good an order to the cognitive power. The form is the source of the irradiation coming forth from clarity. Clarity, luminousness, is of the essence of beauty. The one, the integrity of the being that is beautiful, adds to being the notion of being indivisible. Things are what they are, not something else. They possess their own unity, manifested by their internal order. Things must stay within their own limits of what they are, otherwise there is no whole. Part of the essence of beauty is precisely that the parts of things remain what they are as parts, so that the proportion and order appear.

VI

There are beautiful things, and we perceive them, know them, and rejoice that they exist. We cannot doubt this initial, observed experience that everywhere confronts us even when we least expect it. Beauty is not an inner creation of our minds subsequently projected onto reality. Were this the case, we would never confront anything but ourselves. Our whole being responds to *what is*, to what is there that strikes us. Much of modern thought rightly sees in beauty a danger to its own philosophic principles, rooted as they often are in relativism or idealism. Beauty is from outside of us; even, as in Augustine's case, when it is found within us, it is not of our own initial making. What is found within us, on self-reflection, is not precisely ourselves, not something of our own construction. We are taken to what caused ourselves to be what we are in the first place.

We are, in some sense, mysterious, even to ourselves. Jacques Maritain, reflecting on the relation of mystery to beauty, wrote, "There is in fact no mystery where there is *nothing to know*: mystery exists where there is *more to be known* than is given in our comprehension. To define the beautiful by the radiance of the form is in reality to define it by the radiance of its mystery."[9] The very fact that we exist as we are portends an awareness of what can cause anything to exist so that each encountered being touches this mystery of "more to be known" in a different form. It is characteristic of our encounter especially with beautiful things that, rejoicing or being struck by what they are, we cannot leave what we do not yet know alone.

[9]Jacques Maritain, *Art and Scholasticism* (Notre Dame: University of Notre Dame Press, 1974), 28n.

"Beauty is essentially an object of *intelligence*," this same Jacques Maritain wrote in his discussion of "Art and Beauty" in *Art and Scholasticism*, "for that which *knows* in the full sense of the word is intelligence, which alone is open to the infinity of being. The natural place of beauty is the intelligible world; it is from there that it descends. But it also, in a way, falls under the grasp of the sense, in so far as in man they serve the intelligence and can themselves take delight in knowing."[10] This description is another way of saying that the full comprehension of the beauty of a thing depends on our knowing all its levels, all its particulars, such that all our knowing powers are to be employed. The mind, as Aristotle defined it, is precisely that power in us that is *capax omnium*, capable of knowing all things, even if it does not yet know them and must learn of them gradually.

But when Maritain said that "beauty is essentially an object of intelligence", he alerted us to the relation of beauty and truth. We can say that something is one or itself in its inner order, that it is this thing, not that. We can also say that this same thing is true in that what it is can be known by minds. We can say that this same thing is good in that it can be desired by some will and sought out by it. But each thing is also beautiful, which is a transcendental predicate likewise applicable to *all that is*, a reminder that all things "delight us". We sometimes forget why this latter notion of being pleased or delighted is so significant and why someone like Plato would see why it is so important.

"Like the one, the true and the good, the beautiful is *being* itself considered from a certain aspect", Maritain wrote.

[10] Ibid., 23.

> It is a property of being. It is not an accident superadded to being; it adds to being only a relation of reason; it is being considered as delighting, by the mere intuition of it, an intellectual nature. Thus everything is beautiful, just as everything is good, at least in a certain relation. And as being is everywhere present and everywhere varied the beautiful is likewise diffused everywhere and is everywhere varied.[11]

This passage is the great manifesto against those who find the world dull and boring. Everywhere we look and everything we hear is a reminder of the variety of *what is*, not only its variety but its capacity to delight us. In this sense, we can say we are made open to the beautiful in order precisely that we be delighted in things. This capacity is the very structure of our being.

We are capable not only of knowing or beholding what is beautiful, but in our own way, of creating—or better—making it. This constitutes the final order of which Aquinas spoke, the order we, with our own minds and hands, put into things. We are confronted in the history of the world not only with natural things, our own actions or our own mind, but with things of our own art or craft. The word "art", in its classical sense, refers primarily not to what is made but to the capacity and acquired habit of making what does not exist. This explains the great analogy between God as an artist in making the cosmos, itself an order, and man's making of beautiful things, things for their own sakes. We are not only beings who know and receive, but also beings who, on receiving and knowing, can imitate, make what exists to be something more beautiful than it is. This was the point of Samuel Johnson's observation about the beautiful design on the useful teacup. This

[11] Ibid., 30.

artistic and craft capacity that we have as human beings is in some fundamental sense the response of beauty to beauty.

Aquinas points out that what is good is "diffusive" of itself. He does not mean by this that God, in His goodness, was determined to create, as if He were necessitated to so by something in or outside of Himself. On the other hand, we cannot deny the possibility of the Good, in the sense of the trinitarian Godhead, producing from nothing what is also not God but good. When Maritain noted the relation between the varied diffusion of the good in the universe, he likewise indicated the diffusion of what is beautiful in all its variety.

Armand Maurer, in one of the best books on beauty—again to bring up a rather heavy philosophic point that I want to clarify here—wrote, "The study of beauty, then, falls within metaphysics, or ontology. It is that part of metaphysics devoted to the study of the transcendent property of being whereby it gives pleasure to one who apprehends it. Aesthetics, understood as the study of sensual beauty and its properties, is a part of the ontology of beauty."[12] Beauty refers to that whole aspect of something *that is* that simply gives pleasure to who knows it, to who encounters it. This is a remarkable aspect of reality. It is not just that we can know all things, but they can and do delight us, as if we were being constantly given a gift of what is not ourselves.

If we attempt to apply this aspect to the Godhead, namely, "God is beautiful", it puts us in a different mode. We do not become gods, nor do we consume the wholeness of the Godhead. But we are delighted that God is God and that what He is, his internal trinitarian order, really stands

[12] Armand A. Maurer, *About Beauty: A Thomist Interpretation* (Houston: Center for Thomistic Studies, 1983), 34.

outside of nothingness. Even though we cannot compare our own delight to that of either God Himself or the angels, or even to the holier of our kind, still we can rejoice in what exists, knowing that it could never be if it depended on us. And we are likewise aware that we ourselves contain within us this same radiance that is proper to all beings. And it is in this that we remember Plato's prayer that we become beautiful inside and outside, as if to say, as the tractates on morals do say, that we have to take part in making ourselves beautiful according to that beauty that is handed down to us.

VII

One further point, perhaps, can be made about the order of beauty. When Chesterton used the famous quip that "if a thing is worth doing, it is worth doing badly", the example he used to illustrate what he meant was dancing. This is mindful of Chesterton's own comment on seeing the beauty of what appear at first to be ugly or ungainly things. He suggested as examples such things as English roads and wild gardens, or even such persons as Samuel Johnson, who had beautiful souls in very odd-shaped bodies. Ugliness, of course, always portends both our awareness of what is in fact deficient in the form or shape of a thing, but also a promise of what it might be. This is true of moral ugliness as well as physical ugliness.

But when Chesterton used dancing as his example of something worthwhile doing even if done badly, his point was that we do not want everything to be done for us by someone else. Dancing is not one of those things we can really turn over to another. Chesterton was not denying that there are many in the world who cannot dance well. No doubt, dancing is something that most people can learn to do tolerably well. And dance, along with sculpture, music, and painting, is also one of the recognized fine arts, the arts whose primary purpose is simply beauty. Dance too is an art, an acquired habit, something we have to do badly before we can do it well. Someone never willing to dance badly will be someone who never learns to dance at all.

In his commentary on the *Metaphysics* of Aristotle, we find the following remark of Aquinas: "For there are many things which can be moved by themselves, but not in the same way in which they are moved by art, as is clear in the case of dancing. For men who do not have the art of dancing [that is, who dance 'badly'] can move about but not in the way in which men do who do have this art" (1439). Basically, we would prefer to dance well, even when we have to dance badly to learn to dance well. And we should prefer dancing badly to not dancing at all, as otherwise we should miss out altogether on what dancing is, which was Chesterton's point.

One of the great lessons of the history of philosophy has been the record of man's effort to react properly to beauty, including the divine beauty. Many candidates for this way of our reacting have been proposed—song, music, word, images, even dancing. In the tradition of Catholic Christianity in particular, all of these ways have been combined, through the content and context of the liturgy. Here these responses are expressed as something that needed to be first given to us. "The Catholic liturgy is the liturgy of the Word made flesh—made flesh for the sake of the resurrection", Joseph Ratzinger wrote. "And ... it is a cosmic liturgy. Thus it is clear that not only do the human body and signs from the cosmos play an essential role in the liturgy but that matter of this world is part of the liturgy."[13]

This liturgy is also beautiful, both in itself and in the art that has been used to emphasize what is happening. The connection of cosmos and liturgy is intended to suggest that reaction to the divine beauty always, however it appears, results in awe and delight, whether this reaction is to the magnificence of the heavens or to what is happening in the liturgy, the sacrifice of the Word made flesh. C. S. Lewis has expressed much of this point in his famous passage in *Perelandra* about the Great Dance in which he describes the reaction of all creatures to their final awareness of *what is*, of the divine beauty. What is pleasing also tends to come forth in a kind of finite response of gaiety, which seeks to make our world as beautiful as it can in imitation of the beauty *that is*.

> The Great Dance does not wait to be perfect until the peoples of the Low Worlds are gathered into it. We speak not of when it will begin. It has begun from before always. There was no time when we did not rejoice before His face as now. The dance which we dance is at the center and for this dance all things were made. Blessed be He! . . . All is righteousness and there is no equality. Not as when stones lie side by side, but as when stones support and are supported in an arch, such is His order; rule and obedience, begetting and bearing, heat glancing down, life growing up. Blessed be He![14]

There is an "order" to the dancing, to the response of the differing beings in creation. The dance is at the "center", and for this "all things are made".

[13] Ratzinger, *Spirit of the Liturgy*, 220.

[14] C. S. Lewis, *Perelandra* (New York: Macmillan, [1944] 1965), 214.

The "order of beauty", in conclusion, brings us back to its initial and classical definition, *quod visum, placet.* When something pleases us in this sense, we do not wish to change it. We want it to remain what it is. The "great dance" does not result from changing that to whom "Blessed be He" is addressed, but in rejoicing that *it is*. Josef Pieper spelled this point out in another way, one that takes us back ultimately to the internal order in the Godhead. "The traditional name for the utmost perfection to which man may attain, the fulfillment of his being, is *visio beatifica*, the 'seeing that confers bliss'", Pieper wrote in his essay "What Is a Feast?"

> The highest intensification of life, the absolutely perfect activity, the final stilling of all volition, and the partaking of the utmost fullness that life can offer takes place as a kind of seeing; more precisely, that all this is achieved in seeing awareness of the divine ground of the universe.
>
> Incidentally, the tradition in which this view may be found extends much further back than the Christian centuries, perhaps back beyond historical time altogether. A few generations before Plato, the Greek Anaxagoras, in answer to the question of what he had been born for, replied: "For seeing." And in Plato's *Symposium*, Diotima clearly expresses the traditional wisdom of the *visio beatifica*: "This is that life above all others which man should live, in the contemplation of divine beauty; this makes man immortal."[15]

The order of things is directed to the order of beauty. We are born for "seeing" in all its meanings this divine beauty. We respond to it with all our being, the great dance before the "divine ground of the universe".

[15] *Josef Pieper: An Anthology* (San Francisco: Ignatius Press, 1989), 150.

CONCLUSION

> But the One retains all ultimate authority, and (or so it seems as viewed in serial time) reserves the right to intrude the finger of God into the story: that is to produce realities which could not be deduced even from a complete knowledge of the previous past, but which being real become part of the effective past for all subsequent time.
>
> —J. R. R. Tolkien, letter to Michael Straight, January 1956[1]

The many orders of reality intersect. In a 1954 *Peanuts* comic strip, we see a little girl chasing Charlie Brown, who is running for his life with a magazine. He suddenly stops with the magazine held behind his back but looks directly at the furious girl. She says angrily, "If you don't give me that comic magazine, I'll hit you over the head with it!" With a sudden intelligent look on his face, Charlie replies, "If I don't give you this comic magazine, how are you going to hit me over the head with it?" The final scene simply shows Charlie running for his life with the angry girl in hot pursuit. He says, in self-justification, "I think that was very logical!"

And, of course, it was a very logical statement. *Nemo dat quod non habet*—no one gives what he does not have. No one can hit Charlie if he does not have anything to hit him with. But the "order of logic" does not deter the little girl from pursuing what she intends to have. She still intends to

[1] *The Letters of J. R. R. Tolkien*, edited by Humphrey Carpenter (Boston: Houghton Mifflin, 1981), 235.

bonk Charlie over the head when she catches him. We are logical beings; our minds have order. We are also acting beings, seeking order of soul. We do not know whether this scene involves a question of justice—that is, whether the magazine is rightly the little girl's and Charlie has taken it away from her—or a question of raw desire. She just wants it. She wants it whether it is hers or not. All of these orders and more, as we have seen, exist and need to be understood and related to each other.

In Pascal's well known *Pensées* we find numerous subheadings such as "Glory", "Contradiction", "Perpetuity", "Morality", and "Types". Among these subheadings, the word "Order" appears some seven times, always somewhat enigmatically. "I would have far more fear of being mistaken," Pascal writes, "and of [subsequently] finding that the Christian religion was true, than of not being mistaken in believing it true" (241). Why, we wonder, does he entitle this passage precisely "Order"? At first sight, he is talking about fear, a passion, not order, which is a thing of the mind in which we see how things are related to one another. But, of course, the very meaning of ethics is to put order into our passions so that they can properly be what they are. Fear of the Lord or of anything that is worthy of fear is a good thing.

Obviously, as in the case of Charlie Brown's logic, we need to be alert to the logic contained in what Pascal has written. He states things negatively, always tricky to comprehend logically. He obviously has his famous wager in mind, about not taking a chance that Christianity might just be true and the subsequent high cost of losing the wager if he bets that it isn't. The consequences are too grave. Order here means playing the odds. The first "mistake" or alternative thus consists in thinking Christianity is *not* true, when in fact it is true. This mistake, when carried out, means that I have the whole picture of the world wrong. Christianity had it right, and I bet against it. In this case, with me wrong and Christianity right, I fear not only for my soul but also for my mind.

If, however, I am not mistaken and from the beginning hold that Christianity is true, I have less fear. Why so? Presumably because, in this latter case, all I have to worry about are my sins and hell, the reality of both of which I affirm and expect to have to deal with. The worst I can do is choose to lose my own soul—no mean consequence, to be sure. But my view of the world is correct. I understand what I am doing and what reality is about. When I choose to do something of ultimate and dire consequence, no one can maintain that I was not warned, that I did not know what the real world was like in which I lived. My mind is conformed to what really exists, even when I use my mind badly.

The primary functions of intelligence are to notice, articulate, and affirm "the order in things", in things large and in things small. In Psalm 94, we read, "Can he who made the ear, not hear? Can he who made the eye, not see? Will he who corrects nations, not punish? Will he who teaches men, not have knowledge?" If we answer no to these design questions, we must still account for hearing, seeing, judging, and knowing as if they had no other cause but themselves.

But that alternative will not do either, because hearing, seeing, judging, and thinking cannot as such, since we know them to be already existing, come from nothing. Or else we must deny that they exist at all, even though we use them every day. They are an illusion. No relationship between mind and reality exists, for without our senses and our mind, we cannot know any reality not ourselves. J. M. Bochenski put the problem well when speaking of laws discovered by existing minds:

> When an engineer plans a bridge, he relies on a great number of physical laws. Now, if one would assume, as Hume does, that all of these laws are only habits of mankind, or more precisely of this engineer, then one must ask how it is possible that a bridge which is correctly planned according to the proper laws will stand solid, whereas one in whose planning the engineer has made mistakes will fall apart. How can human habits be decisive for such masses of concrete and iron? It seems as if the laws are only secondarily in the mind of the engineer. Primarily they are valid *for the world*, for iron and concrete, totally independently of whether anyone knows something about them or not.[2]

The order already exists in things. We come to know what this order is. We come to use it because it is really in things. We do not make the order or the law. Rather, we discover it, and subsequently we can use it for our purposes.

So we have found that the pursuit of understanding yields some knowledge of order, of what it is. The order within the Godhead, in the cosmos, in the soul, in the polity, in the mind, and even in hell, together with the order of redemption and of beauty, open us to what is not ourselves. But in doing so, it illuminates us to ourselves. We know most about ourselves when, at the same time, we know what is not ourselves. "Not only nature has its orders, its forms of life that we have to heed if we want to live by and in it," Joseph Cardinal Ratzinger wrote, "man too is essentially a creature and has a creaturely order. He can't

[2] J. M. Bochenski, *Philosophy: An Introduction* (New York: Harper Torchbooks, 1972), 13–14.

arbitrarily make anything he wants of himself."[3] The orders of cosmos, soul, mind, polity, and of making are everywhere to be encountered.

In another of Pascal's "order" entries, in a section dealing with the Fall, we read, "It is right that all those who are in that [fallen] state should know it, both those who are content with it, and those who are not content with it; but it is not right that all should see Redemption" (no. 449). All should, in other words, know that there is something wrong with the human condition, even though there is something right about it. Original sin, Chesterton once remarked, is the one doctrine that needs no "proof", for all we need to do to see it is "to go out in the streets and open our eyes." Fallen man can know that there is something wrong with his condition, with doing "what he would not", as Saint Paul put it. But, on this basis alone, he may have no awareness or hope of any possibility of some other way in which he can deal with his disorders or escape from them.

It is right that all should be offered redemption. But this offer cannot come from men themselves, as if they were sufficient to deal with the depths of the problem in their own souls with the sole aid of their own powers and resources. Indeed, the claim to do so is, throughout history, the key rebellion that man puts into the world. This is the effort to create an order other than that given through nature and redemption. This has historically gone by the name of "pride". In the end, there is no "self-redemption", only repentance once redemption is offered. And the "rightness" of the offer is not human rightness.

[3] Joseph Cardinal Ratzinger, *Salt of the Earth* (San Francisco: Ignatius Press, 1997), 231.

It is not "right" that all should see redemption without first its including the freedom of each to choose or accept it. There is no automatic redemption from the order that includes man's freedom, even his freedom to sin and initiate disorder in the various orders of being. God does not automatically redeem us. The purpose of redemption is to restore the original design of creation to associate other free beings, in their freedom, in the inner life of the Godhead. It is this purpose that governs the order of human things in their relation to the order within the Godhead.

In his *Autobiographical Reflections*, Eric Voegelin, the great philosopher of order and history, recalled that he was often asked about the meaning of order and disorder in his writings. He replied,

> The reality of order is not my discovery. I am speaking of the order in reality discovered by mankind as far back as we have any written records, and now even farther back as we become familiar with the symbols in monuments discovered by archeologists as far back as the Paleolithicum. By *order* is meant the structure of reality as experienced as well as the attunement of man to an order that is not of his making—i.e., the cosmic order.[4]

There is order in the cosmos, as well as order in our minds in knowing and being attuned to this cosmos.

Within this same cosmos, we are already what we are. We are already more glorious than any other model that we try to impose on our actual being. We have by our nature the ability both to know and to make. We likewise have the ability and the responsibility to order ourselves

[4] Eric Voegelin, *Autobiographical Reflections* (Baton Rouge: Louisiana State University Press, 1989), 76.

and our cities, the very capacity to "do", which implies the power to disorder ourselves and our cities. The order we put into things under our guidance is a free order, one with consequences. It is free in the sense not of our making what it is by ourselves, but in freely accepting it as already our purpose.

In the letter to Michael Straight cited at the beginning of this chapter, J. R. R. Tolkien speaks of the fact that we can also encounter things in reality that we cannot deduce from a clear knowledge of past things. That is to say, as we understand in considering redemption, realities exist in the world that are not "caused" by what we know of the world by our own powers, yet we really encounter them. They abide, are handed down, are remembered. Such is the presence of revelation as itself an unexpected but no less real and coherent order to which our minds are open, but not on our own terms.

To deny this openness to the principles and events of revelation on the grounds that they are beyond our reason is what is classically defined as "rationalism", the very opposite of the sort of understanding of mind and reality that we find in Aristotle and Plato, even though neither, technically speaking, ever directly encountered the revelation to the Gentiles that Saint Paul spoke of. That all of these orders are related in a whole so that the understanding of one leads to and completes the other is the thesis of this book.

In conclusion, it seems fitting to cite a remark of Chesterton that serves to remind us of what is at stake in recognizing the distinction in things. It is important that things be what they are, however related to the whole they are. It is likewise important that we know both what things are and that they are distinct. "No other philosophy makes God actually rejoice in the separation of the universe into living souls. But according to orthodox Christianity this separation between God and man is sacred, because this is eternal. That a man may love God it is necessary that there should be not only a God to be loved, but a man to love him."[5] In the end, it is, perhaps, no longer necessary to point out both the logic and the wisdom in those distinctions between God and man within *the order of things*.

[5] G.K. Chesterton, *Orthodoxy* (San Francisco: Ignatius Press, [1908] 1995), 139.

SELECT BIBLIOGRAPHY

The following bibliography does not include the basic works of Plato, Aristotle, Augustine, Aquinas, and other "great thinkers". It is assumed that these works are already known and easily available. Here, rather, are selected books that, in one way or another, argue to one or another of the issues of order that are found in the text.

Belloc, Hilaire. *The Path to Rome.* San Francisco: Ignatius Press, 2003.

Bochenski, J. M. *Philosophy—An Introduction.* New York: Harper Torchbooks, 1972.

Boswell, James. *Boswell's Life of Johnson.* London: Oxford, 1931. 2 vols.

Butterfield, Herbert. *Christianity and History.* London: Fontana, 1957.

Catechism of the Catholic Church. Second Edition. Rome: Liberia Editrice Vaticana, 1997.

Chesterton, G. K. *Orthodoxy.* San Francisco: Ignatius Press, [1908] 1995.

———. *What's Wrong with the World.* San Francisco: Ignatius Press, [1910] 1994.

Dawson, Christopher. *Religion and the Rise of Western Culture.* Garden City: Doubleday Image, 1958.

De Lubac, Henri. *Catholicism: Christ and the Common Destiny of Man.* San Francisco: Ignatius Press, [1947] 1988.

Derrick, Christopher. *Escape from Skepticism: Liberal Education as If the Truth Really Mattered*. San Francisco: Ignatius Press, 2005.

Fortin, Ernest L. *Collected Works*. Lanham, Md.: Rowman and Littlefield, 1996. 3 vols.

Gilson, Étienne. *God and Philosophy*. New Haven: Yale University Press, 1941.

_____. *The Unity of Philosophical Experience*. San Francisco: Ignatius Press, [1937] 1999.

Guardini, Romano. *The End of the Modern World*. Wilmington: ISI Books, [1956] 1998.

Howard, Thomas. *Chance or the Dance?* San Francisco: Ignatius Press, 1989.

Jaki, Stanley L. *Chance or Reality*. Wilmington: ISI Books, 1986.

_____. *The Road of Science and the Ways of God*. Chicago: University of Chicago Press, 1978.

Johnson, Samuel. *Selected Essays*. Harmondsworth: Penguin, 2003.

Kraut, Richard. *Aristotle: Political Philosophy*. London: Oxford, 2002.

Kraynak, Robert P. *Christian Faith and Modern Democracy: God and Democracy in a Fallen World*. Notre Dame: University of Notre Dame Press, 2001.

Kreeft, Peter. *Back to Virtue*. San Francisco: Ignatius Press, 1992.

_____. *The Philosophy of Tolkien*. San Francisco: Ignatius Press, 2005.

Leiva-Merikakis, Erasmo. *Love's Sacred Order: The Four Loves Revisited*. San Francisco: Ignatius Press, 2000.

Lewis, C. S. *Mere Christianity*. New York: Macmillan, 1952.

McCoy, Charles N. R. *The Structure of Political Thought*. New York: Macmillan, 1963.

McInerny, Ralph. *The Very Special Hours of Jacques Maritain.* Notre Dame: University of Notre Dame Press, 2003.
McIntyre, Alasdair. *After Virtue.* Notre Dame: University of Notre Dame Press, 1981.
Maritain, Jacques. *Art and Scholasticism.* Notre Dame: University of Notre Dame Press, 1974.
_____. *Man and the State.* Chicago: University of Chicago Press, 1951.
Mascall, E. L. *The Christian Universe.* London: Longman, Darton, and Todd, 1966.
_____. *Grace and Glory.* Denville, N.J.: Dimension, 1961.
Maurer, Armand A. *About Beauty: A Thomistic Interpretation.* Houston: Center for Thomistic Studies, 1983.
Morse, Jennifer Roback. *Love and Economics.* Dallas: Spence, 2001.
Navone, John. *Towards a Theology of Beauty.* Collegeville, Minn.: Liturgical Press, 1996.
Newman, John Henry. *Parochial and Plain Sermons.* San Francisco: Ignatius Press, 1997.
O'Connor, Flannery. *The Habit of Being.* New York: Vintage, 1979.
Pickstock, Catherine. *After Writing: On the Liturgical Consummation of Philosophy.* Oxford: Blackwell, 1997.
Pieper, Josef. *In Defense of Philosophy.* San Francisco: Ignatius Press, 1992.
_____. *In Tune with the World.* Chicago: Franciscan Herald, 1972.
_____. *Josef Pieper: An Anthology.* San Francisco: Ignatius Press, 1989.
_____. *Living the Faith: The Truth of Things and Reality and the Good.* San Francisco: Ignatius Press, 1989.
Quinn, Dennis. *Iris Exiled: A Synoptic History of Wonder.* Lanham, Md.: University Press of America, 2002.

Ratzinger, Joseph Cardinal [Benedict XVI]. *Introduction to Christianity*. San Francisco: Ignatius Press, 2004.

______. *Salt of the Earth: The Church at the End of the Millennium: An Interview with Peter Seewald*. San Francisco: Ignatius Press, 1997.

______. *The Spirit of the Liturgy*. San Francisco: Ignatius Press, 2000.

Reilly, Robert R. *Surprised by Beauty*. Washington: Morley Books, 2002.

Rowland, Tracey. *Culture and the Thomist Tradition*. London: Routledge, 2003.

Saward, John. *The Beauty of Holiness and the Holiness of Beauty*. San Francisco: Ignatius Press, 1996.

Sayers, Dorothy. *The Man Born to Be King*. San Francisco: Ignatius Press [1943] 1990.

Schall, James V. *At the Limits of Political Philosophy*. Washington: Catholic University of America Press, 1996.

______. *The Life of the Mind: On the Joys and Travails of Thinking*. Wilmington: ISI Books, 2006.

______. *On the Unseriousness of Human Affairs*. Wilmington: ISI Books, 2001.

______. *Redeeming the Time*. New York: Sheed and Ward, 1968.

______. *Schall on Chesterton: Timely Essays on Timeless Paradoxes*. Washington: Catholic University of America Press, 2000.

______. *The Sum Total of Human Happiness*. South Bend, Ind.: St. Augustine's Books, 2006.

______. *What Is God Like?* Collegeville, Minn.: Liturgical Press / Michael Glazier, 1992.

Schumacher, E. F. *A Guide for the Perplexed*. New York: Harper Colophon, 1977.

Sertillanges, A. D. *The Intellectual Life*. Washington: Catholic University of America Press, 1998.

Simon, Yves. *A General Theory of Authority*. Notre Dame: University of Notre Dame Press, 1980.

Sokolowski, Robert. *Christian Faith and Human Understanding*. Washington: Catholic University of America Press, 2006.

———. *Eucharistic Presence*. Washington: Catholic University of America Press, 1993.

———. *The God of Faith and Reason*. Washington: Catholic University of America Press, 1995.

Strauss, Leo. *The City and Man*. Chicago: University of Chicago Press, 1964.

Tolkien, J. R. R. *The Letters of J. R. R. Tolkien*. Boston: Houghton Mifflin, 1981.

Veatch, Henry B. *Aristotle: A Contemporary Appreciation*. Bloomington: Indiana University Press, 1974.

———. *Rational Man: A Modern Interpretation of Aristotelian Ethics*. Bloomington: Indiana University Press, 1966.

Voegelin, Eric. *Conversations with Eric Voegelin*. Montreal: Thomas More Institute Papers, 1980.

Von Balthasar, Hans Urs. *Convergences: To the Source of Christian Mystery*. Trans. E. A. Nelson. San Francisco: Ignatius Press, 1983.

Wallace, William A. *The Modelling of Nature: Philosophy of Science and Philosophy of Nature in Synthesis*. Washington: Catholic University of America Press, 1996.

Walsh, David. *The Third Millennium: Reflections on Faith and Reason*. Washington: Georgetown University Press, 1999.

Wojtyla, Karol [John Paul II]. *Crossing the Threshold of Hope*. New York: Knopf, 1994.

———. *Memory and Identity*. New York: Rizzoli, 2003.

INDEX